FLYING SOLDIERS

FLYING SOLDIERS

Tim Lambert

BBC BOOKS

Picture Credits

BBC Books would like to thank the following for providing photographs and for granting permission to reproduce them in this book: Angus Beaton (pages 8, 14, 44, 49, 50, 180, 181, 185), Tim Lambert (pages 72, 81, 169), McDonnell Douglas Aerospace Inc. (page 11), and Touch Productions Ltd (pages 55, 60, 61, 67).

This book is published to accompany the television series entitled *Flying Soldiers* which was first broadcast in 1995.
The series was produced by Touch Productions Ltd
Executive Producer: Malcolm Brinkworth
Producer: Will Aslett
Director: Tim Lambert

Published by BBC Books,
an imprint of BBC Worldwide Publishing.
BBC Worldwide Limited, Woodlands,
80 Wood Lane, London W12 0TT

First published 1995

ISBN 0 563 37127 7

Designed by Andrew Shoolbred

Photographs by Justin Pumfrey

Set in 10/13pt Palatino

Printed and bound in Great Britain by Butler & Tanner Ltd,
Frome and London
Colour separations by Radstock Reproductions, Midsomer Norton
Jacket printed by Lawrence Allen Ltd, Weston-super-Mare

Contents

Acknowledgements

This is the first book I have ever written, and my thanks go to Sheila Ableman at BBC Books for being brave enough to give me the opportunity. The editors Kelly Davies and Khadija Manjlai have worked hard to get the text into shape, but I fear I have tested their patience to breaking point. Thank you for bearing with me.

I am indebted to everyone who worked on the television series, particularly our regular cameramen Tony Miller, Roger Chapman and Steve Robinson, and our sound recordist Kevin Meredith. In the office, Gina Hobson and Jacqui Loton made sure the operation ran smoothly. In the cutting room, John Seymour and Julian Kyle worked long hours with great professionalism. Malcolm Brinkworth and Steve Hewlett were executive producers, and both helped shape the storyline of the series. But two individuals have done most to make this project a success: firstly, Stephen Singleton, the film editor, who has been endlessly patient and good-natured. He turned ten miles of film into three hours of coherent television, which was no small achievement. Secondly, Will Aslett, the producer, who kept the show on the road for a year and a half. He has a rare talent for bringing out the best in people.

I would also like to thank everyone at the School of Army Aviation who made us so welcome for a year and tolerated our media ways. At the risk of offending others, I would like to single out Major General Simon Lyttle, Colonel Tony McMahon, Colonel Mike Wawn, Lieutenant Colonel David Patterson, Major John Lay, Major Bruce Stewart, Captain Nick Wharmby, Fred Trowern, Bob Weston, Sam Law, and WO2 Kyle Webster. All of them helped us at different stages of the project and gave every assistance with the filming. Special thanks go to our long-suffering liaison officer, Captain Nigel Brain. He was a great fixer, who kept his sense of humour through the most trying moments. He is now leaving the Army and I wish him well in his new career as a lawyer. Finally, I would like to thank the trainees on Course 354. Without them nothing would have been possible.

Introduction

Ten Green Pilots

Since the year dot, man has looked at the birds and tried to fly. Icarus strapped on a pair of wings but flew too near the sun and met a rather messy end. For just as long, man has waged war, usually with more success. Before he could speak, he learned to fight.

But it's only in the last hundred years that these two passions have been combined. The twentieth century is the first in which soldiers have found ways of fighting in the air. After sticks, swords, guns and boats, the military aircraft was a logical development. But no one could have predicted the extent to which air power has transformed the way wars are fought. It is now a truism to say that 'he who dominates the air, dominates the battlefield'. The Gulf War, for example, was a conflict fought and won by hi-tech fighter planes and helicopters.

The Army Air Corps is the Army's flying wing. It exists completely separate of the Royal Air Force, and actually flies more aircraft than the RAF. The difference between the two has traditionally been the difference between a fighting arm and a support arm. The RAF attacks the enemy directly, using its own firepower, whereas the Army Air Corps helps other – ground-based – forces engage the enemy. In particular, army pilots, since the First World War, have acted as the eyes of artillery gunners. They are able to climb up high, watch an enemy target and direct fire on to it. These skills are still taught to every new pilot.

But, over the last couple of decades, the difference between the two forces has become blurred. Since the 1970s the Army

An Army Air Corps Lynx (above) flying with its own payload of anti-tank missiles. The Gazelle (opposite) is unarmed, but serves as an ideal platform to observe the enemy.

Air Corps has fitted weapons to some of its aircraft and developed its own aggressive battlefield role, primarily concerned with destroying tanks. This role is gradually being expanded. At the time of writing, the Corps is buying two billion pounds worth of new-generation attack aircraft, designed to find, root out and destroy the enemy without assistance from any other forces.

So if both the Army Air Corps and the RAF are now involved in an attack capacity, what is the difference between them? Put simply, the RAF flies fast jets and the Army Air Corps flies helicopters. It's a difference which has occurred more by accident than design: when helicopters were introduced after the Second World War, they were found to be ideal artillery observation platforms, so the Army Air Corps invested heavily in them, while the RAF focused their attention on fast jet technology. As helicopters have developed, the Army Air

Corps has continued to lead the way in rotary wing flying.

Established as an independent corps in 1957, it has taken its helicopters into two wars, the Falklands and the Gulf, and has established operations all over the world, wherever British interests are at stake – in Belize, Hong Kong, Germany, Cyprus and Bosnia. It has also played a long and significant role in Northern Ireland, moving troops around the province, providing surveillance and sometimes engaging directly with the IRA.

Despite defence cuts, the Air Corps is one of the few branches of the Army which has grown in recent years. The Armed Forces are adjusting to life in the post-Cold War world, and no one is quite sure where future conflicts will arise or how they will be fought. But one thing is certain: versatility and manoeuvrability will be the buzzwords of the future, and no weapon in the military arsenal is more versatile or manoeuvrable than the helicopter. It is fast, agile and potentially lethal. The new two billion pound attack helicopters will be the largest defence procurement ever made in peacetime.

But if helicopters are to become the weapon of the future, helicopter pilots must keep pace with the changes. The Army Air Corps needs to recruit and train pilots who will be able to adapt to the new demands being made of them. The modern pilot is someone with extraordinary flying skills allied to a strong tactical and strategic sense, who can read a battlefield, size up a situation and strike at the right moment. They are looking for thinking aviators, rather than jobbing pilots – hence the idea for *Flying Soldiers*.

We wanted to show how today's Army pilots are trained, by following a group of new recruits from day one of their training to the day of their wings parade. The recruits come from across the ranks and regiments of the Army and they start off knowing nothing about flying. Within a year they have to learn first how to fly a helicopter and then how to command it in battle. The best will go on to be groomed as pilots of the new attack helicopters. Others will fall by the wayside and have to return to their existing jobs at their old bases. The line between success and failure is remarkably thin.

The future of army aviation lies in attack helicopters like the Apache, which dominated the Gulf War. The Army Air Corps is now purchasing its own fleet of attack helicopters.

This is not really a military book – plenty of others have explained the finer points of army

AH64D
LONGBOW

aviation in much more detail and with far greater expertise, and I bow to their superior knowledge. Instead, I have tried to write about the people who go through this training: who they are, what motivates them, and how they deal with failure. It's a story set in a military context, but it deals with emotions that are familiar to everyone: the hopes and fears of ten people chasing a dream.

I'll never forget the moment when the instructor let go of the controls and uttered those fateful words 'you have control'. It was a wet and windy day and the trainees' flying programme had been cancelled, so I decided to take the instructors up on their offer of a free flying lesson. I had never been in a helicopter before starting work on *Flying Soldiers;* now I was piloting one.

The instructor had asked me to hold a hover over a whole field. I thought he was humouring me: it can't be that hard. I was wrong. Ten seconds later my helicopter was scuttling at great speed three fields away. I might have been piloting the aircraft, but I certainly wasn't controlling it. I had more instruction, then another go and another, but the helicopter refused to do what I wanted. Eventually my instructor took over again, and the unruly machine immediately stopped playing up. It seemed so unfair. By way of consolation, he told me that he'd recently taken one of the top Concorde pilots for a ride and he'd fared no better.

I returned to base with a mixture of emotions: excitement at having made my first flight in the pilot's seat, frustration at doing so badly and determination to get another go. I had only flown for three-quarters of an hour but I felt exhausted, physically and mentally. My brain was in overload, replaying moments from the flight and admonishing myself for doing so badly. And for the first time I understood what it must be like to learn to fly, that rollercoaster ride between elation and self-doubt. Add the pressure of knowing that your career depends on the outcome of each flight, and I realized what the trainee pilots must feel every day of the course.

The centre for all Air Corps training is the School of Army Aviation at Middle Wallop in Hampshire. It is a small unremarkable base, dominated by five imposing green hangars which house the aircraft. It adjoins a vast grassy airfield, which on a busy day sees more take-offs and landings than Heathrow. What is immediately noticeable about the base is its rather unmilitary atmosphere. There's very little saluting and marching, and almost no shouting. I started the project expecting to film lots of people barking orders and delivering hell-and-damnation reprimands when things go wrong – the stuff of most military documentaries. But the longer I stayed on the base, the longer I waited. Here the soldiers are treated as adults. They are encouraged to take the initiative and think things out for themselves. The Army Air Corps has come to the conclusion that flying and shouting don't mix.

Middle Wallop is a pilot factory – every seven weeks a new course of trainee pilots start on the conveyor belt. Once the go-ahead for the *Flying Soldiers* project had been given, it was a matter of deciding which course we were to follow. Eventually, the demands of the television commissioning process dictated that we start filming in February 1994, which meant Course 354 would be the lucky group.

The ten soldiers earmarked for the course were informed of the dubious privilege that awaited them: they were to have a film crew following their every move. The Corps gave them all an option to pull out, but only two did because of Ulster connections and an understandable camera shyness. The other eight agreed to the filming, but for most of them it felt like Hobson's Choice. They'd all waited such a long time to get their places; if they declined them now, they had no idea how much longer they might have to wait for another chance.

Less than a week before the course started, another member pulled out – not by choice, but on doctor's orders. He had failed his final medical examination on the grounds of susceptibility to strobe lighting, a fatal weakness for any potential helicopter pilot. He was very distraught at losing his place at the last moment, having spent two years going through the selection process. He vowed that he would get a second opinion from a private doctor and have surgery to his eyes if necessary – anything to get his chance to fly. It was a cruel blow indeed, but it gave us an early insight into how passionately people feel about this course and just how much is riding on it for each one of them.

Course 354: (Back row, from left) Corporal Jim LeCornu, Bombardier Paul Stoneman, Corporal David Rooney, Corporal Mark Hitch, Corporal Nigel Harrison. (Front row) Corporal Marcus Lock, Second Lieutenant Andy James, Lieutenant Jenny Firth, Lieutenant JP Miller, Staff Sergeant Mark Finch.

So Course 354 was left with only seven of its original ten, and three late replacements had to be drafted in from the pool of people scheduled for future courses. The weekend before the course started, I turned up with my producer and camera crew to meet all the trainees for the first time. I found ten rather anxious soldiers – anxious about a year of intense training, but just as anxious about a year of intense filming. The rest of Middle Wallop had already christened them 'The Hollywood Course'. Here is a run-down of the reluctant film stars, in order of rank:

Lieutenant Jenny Firth is the only woman on the course. She has been in the Army for six years, working in administrative, office-based jobs. When she joined up, becoming a military pilot seemed an impossible ambition, but in 1992 the Corps changed its policy and allowed females to fly. She is the fourth woman to be selected for the pilot's course. The other three both passed and moved into operational squadrons; Jenny will be hoping to do the same. She is one of the dreamers on the course. She has wanted to fly since childhood, having lived overseas and spent a lot of time in aeroplanes. She already has a civilian pilot's licence on fixed wing planes, and loves the freedom that flying brings.

Lieutenant John Paul 'JP' Miller is a white Zimbabwean who came to Britain to study and then decided to stay and join the Armed Forces. He did a spell with the RAF, before opting for the Army Air Corps and helicopters. He took all the selection tests and won his place on the course, but his future in the Army is entirely dependent on him passing out; all officers in the Corps must be qualified pilots. If he fails, he'll have to leave and apply to another non-flying regiment or face unemployment. In his case that would mean a change in his immigration status and he might have to return to Zimbabwe. But failure is far from his mind: he's a serious, ambitious young man with a will to succeed.

Second Lieutenant Andy James is the youngest member of the group. At twenty-one, he's only been out of school for three years. Like JP, his future career is dependent on him passing the course. If he fails he has nowhere else to go back to in the Army. Unlike JP, he is in no danger of taking things too seriously. He's determined to enjoy his year at Middle Wallop, and keep smiling through adversity. The Army Air Corps claims that the best pilots have the same character profile, one they call 'stable extrovert'. Andy is certainly the most extrovert member of the group; quite how stable he is will become clearer over the course of the year.

Staff Sergeant Mark Finch is the oldest member of the group. At thirty-two, he has spent half his life in the Army, most of it in the Royal Signals. He comes to the course straight from a posting in Cyprus with the British–UN peacekeeping operation. He is certainly not a dreamer and has no romantic ideas about flying up high with the birds. He is just after a more interesting job and a way of relaunching his career. As the only senior non-commissioned officer in the group, he'll have an important part to play in pulling the course together and acting as a link between the officers and the corporals.

Corporal Mark Hitch has already spent six years in the Army Air Corps as a groundcrewman. Unlike his four seniors, he knows that, even if he fails the course, he still has a future in the Corps and he'll carry on working with aircraft, albeit on the ground rather than in the air. This knowledge gives him a pragmatic attitude. If he passes he'll be happy, if not he'll accept it and continue with his career. His real dream is to work his way up the ranks; he wants to become a sergeant, and then go on to become a sergeant-major. His biggest anxiety about the course is that it might slow down his path to promotion.

Corporal Nigel Harrison is a man with excellent flying credentials. His father is an Air Commodore in the RAF and his two brothers are pilots. They all fly fixed wing planes, but he has opted for helicopters. He didn't have the grades for an officer's commission so he wouldn't have been able to fly in the RAF, but the Army Air Corps has an open policy on rank and has given him the chance to continue in the family tradition. Like Mark Hitch, he already works in the Corps, but in his case as an aircrewman doing back-up duties on Lynx helicopters, and occasionally given responsibility for basic piloting. He is the only member of the group with any previous rotary wing experience and should therefore start with an advantage.

Corporal Marcus Lock is a foot soldier who has served nine years with the Light Infantry. He is the epitome of the cynical, sarcastic squaddie, but underneath his gruff exterior, he is really one of the dreamers. He loves flying and can't wait to take control of a helicopter. He will seize this opportunity to get out of the Infantry and into a more free-thinking environment. He is too opinionated to fit in comfortably with the demands of

Infantry life, and has twice been disciplined for insubordination. He will enjoy the greater freedom enjoyed by pilots.

Bombardier Paul Stoneman is the member of the course who most relishes frontline action. He is from an artillery background, but he has undertaken Commando training and has travelled the world on different exercises. He is controlled, cool and purposeful, and claims to be entirely indifferent to flying itself. He is only interested in helicopters in so far as they will make him more effective on the battlefield.

Corporal Jim LeCornu is the quiet man of the group. He worries that he may be out of his depth on the course. Like Mark Hitch, he is a groundcrewman by trade and is taking a big step up by trying to become a pilot.

Corporal David 'Mickey' Rooney is another of the dreamers. Like Jenny, he has a civilian licence on fixed wing planes, and has wanted to fly since childhood. He is the third of the Army Air Corps groundcrewmen, but he's regarded as one of the brightest young talents in the non-commissioned ranks and was accepted for training as soon as he had served the minimum four-year requirement. He is also one of the extroverts on the course and is likely to smile through any setback. Like Andy, he is determined to enjoy himself over the next year. The rest of the group will have to get used to jokes delivered in a thick Glaswegian accent.

Ten soldiers from different backgrounds with different expectations. For the film crew and myself, meeting them all for the first time, it was hard not to speculate about what would happen. How would they cope with the pressure and who would end up collecting their wings? We felt like fortune tellers making predictions about the coming year. But inevitably things were to unfold in ways we could never have imagined.

At this stage the 'we' and 'I' in this book disappear. This is not a story about me or my film crew. It's the story of the ten would-be pilots on Course 354. My job now is to drift into the background and observe. This is what I saw.

Chapter One

Airborne

Monday, 21 February

Middle Wallop, Hampshire

The morning is cold, misty and snowy. The snow is a surprise. It appeared overnight, a white blanket covering the airfield. Normally by now the sky would be buzzing with helicopters taking off, hovering and flying. But today it's quiet; all aircraft are grounded. Even the birds have given up. They seem happier just sitting on the bare branches of the trees. It's an auspicious day for a new start.

'Welcome to Wallop. Congratulations. You've made it this far because we believe you've got what it takes to be Army pilots. And, to prove it, we'll be spending quarter of a million pounds training each of you.' The words are spoken by Colonel Mike Wawn, the Commandant at the School of Army Aviation. He's addressing an audience of ten nervous trainees, on the first day of their pilot's course.

Each of them has been through a long selection process: initial aptitude testing, a strict medical examination, written exams, a formal interview, and thirteen hours of assessed flying. Ninety-five per cent of applicants have been weeded out by now, so these ten trainees represent the elite: those thought to have the right stuff. 'We can teach anyone to fly a helicopter, but only a special person can fly to our needs: flying low in enemy terrain, avoiding radar and dodging bullets.... We want people who can handle pressure – extreme pressure.' The briefing inspires confidence and dread in equal proportion.

As the trainees leave the lecture hall, they realize just what they're embarking upon. For the next year they will be living here at Middle Wallop. Five days a week, for fifty-two weeks, they'll be in the air or in the classroom, assessed every step of the way. If they fall behind, they'll be placed on review. If they can't catch up, quickly, they'll be 'chopped' (military slang for failing). The Corps calls it the toughest course in the Army, and the trainees are beginning to find out why. It's not tough in the traditional military sense – yomping over Dartmoor, digging trenches, and pounding a drill square – but it is tough psychologically. You've got to think, plan and react, while keeping control of a million-pound machine. As Colonel Wawn puts it: 'We'll teach you to fly at 2 miles a minute, but we'll teach you to think at 4 miles a minute.'

First, they need to be kitted out, so it's down to the Quartermaster's Stores. In the Army, the Quartermaster is God. Or, rather, he thinks he's God. He regards all equipment as his own and hands it over with extreme reluctance. One by one, the trainees file in for their flying kit.

'Name?'

'Corporal Hitch.'

'Height, chest size and shoe size?'

'Five foot 9, 42 inches and size 7.'

'Hmm... I'll see what we've got...' The storeman scurries off to examine his stock.

Mark Hitch stands and waits. He's a squaddie and proud of it: 'I never wanted to do anything else.' But he's surprisingly gentle for a squaddie. His soft Cumbrian accent reveals a deep love for his family home in the Lake District. He is also surprisingly nervous: he knows he's not a 'natural flier', and will find the course harder than most. The storeman returns with an armful of kit: overalls, boots, pullover, gloves, T-shirts, helmet. 'Here you go bonny lad, try these on...' He calls everyone 'bonny lad'.

Everyone except Lieutenant Firth. 'Oh hallo, Ma'am...' His demeanour changes dramatically when Jenny Firth arrives in the room. Women are still enough of a rarity in the Army Air Corps for him to play the gentleman. He discreetly omits to ask Jenny for her chest size. She's used to being treated differently; she accepts it as inevitable in a male environment, but she wants to be taken seriously and not thought of as some 'token girlie'. She herself makes few concessions to femininity. On or off duty, she wears no make-up or jewellery and scrapes her long curly hair back off her face, tying it into a tight ponytail. She hopes the Corps are investing 'far too much money in my training to do me any favours'. Unfortunately the storeman doesn't have any size 4 boots: 'They start at 5, because they're meant for men.' He suggests she takes the size 5, wears thick socks and buys an insole.

The last trainee to collect his kit is Second Lieutenant Andy James. He is told off for not having had a helmet-fitting in advance. He apologizes: 'I've been skiing in Switzerland until yesterday. I only came back at the last moment.' Andy is self-confident and charming, always on the lookout for a good time. Life has been kind to him. He enjoyed school – Kings Bruton, a minor public school in Kent – where he played in the first XV. He then deliberated between Sandhurst and university, and chose Sandhurst: 'I looked at architecture and found out it was seven years to do, and I thought that's too long, I'll join the Army and get stuck

They look like relics of a bygone age, but the Chipmunk is a cheap and effective aircraft for teaching basic flying skills.

in straight away.' He took Sandhurst in his stride and was accepted straight into the Army Air Corps, where he's managed to spend as much time skiing as he has soldiering. The previous summer he went parachuting in Dubai – 'just for fun!'

The pilot's course will be the biggest test of character Andy has faced so far. 'I failed A-level biology. That's the only thing in my life I've ever failed – and I'm not expecting to fail this.... If I did fail, I'd be quite upset, but I wouldn't show it at the time. I'd just walk away and cry in my room somewhere.' That's very Andy James: confident of success, but in the event of the unthinkable, he'd keep a stiff upper lip throughout. He wanders over to the helmet workshop where they fit him with a new helmet. As he squeezes his James Dean quiff under the helmet he realizes that sooner or later he'll have to cut it off. Quiffs and military flying don't mix.

One more ritual needs to be completed before the serious work can begin. A photograph is taken of the course. The three officers at the front, Jenny in the middle, the seven non-commissioned officers behind. The sun has burnt off the freezing mist and it's now a crisp winter's afternoon. The trainees have to look straight into the sun as they pose for the camera. Click. Pilot's Course 354 captured in all their anticipation, smiling nervously and squinting.

This group photograph will be framed and put up on every noticeboard in the base. If anyone gets chopped, it is customary to deface the picture with a thick red cross marking out the failed trainee. In this way the photograph acts as a barometer of a course's progress: the greater the number of crosses, the worse the course is doing. At present, Course 354 has only just started and the photograph is free of blemishes. But – the 64 000 dollar question – how many red crosses will have appeared in a year's time?

Monday, 7 March

For two weeks the trainees have been in classrooms, attending briefings and lectures, marking time. But today the flying begins. The Corps describes the course as a series of hurdles – small to begin with, but getting bigger and bigger as the year goes on. The secret is to ignore the complexity of what lies ahead, and look no further than the next hurdle. In this scheme of things, today is hurdle number one – a gentle familiarization flight, a chance for trainee and instructor to get to know each other.

The first phase of training is strictly fixed wing. Before they can set foot inside a helicopter, they must spend two months learning to fly Chipmunks. With its canvas-skinned wings and single propeller, the Chipmunk would look more at home in a museum than on a modern airfield, but the Army Air Corps keeps a small fleet of them in service because they are ideal aircraft to teach the basics of aviation. Whether flying a helicopter or a plane, the skills of navigation, air sense and radio communication are the same, and these skills are taught much more easily and cheaply in a Chipmunk than in a helicopter. However, most of the trainees regard the fixed wing phase as an unwelcome, if necessary, distraction. They're here to fly helicopters, not planes.

At first sight, some of the instructors might also look more at home in a museum. Most of them are ex-RAF pilots who have clocked up thousands of hours in the air, flying everything from fighter planes to Hercules transporters. They have been pensioned out of the RAF but have chosen to sign up with the Army Air Corps as civilian instructors for one simple reason. 'We just love flying. It's a drug,' says Fred Trowern, the Chief Pilot of the Chipmunk fleet. Fred used to be a Wing Commander in the RAF, seeing active service in Aden and the Falklands. Teaching trainees on Chipmunks – top speed 170 knots – may not give the same adrenaline rush as flying a fast jet, but at least he's still in the air. In his spare time, Fred also runs a five-man Chipmunk display team. They call themselves the Grey Owls – combined age of planes, 210 years; combined age of pilots, 310.

It's a beautiful day at Middle Wallop. There's a deep blue sky, the sort of blue you only get in winter when the air is clear of dust. In the distance the first helicopters of the day are taking off, the sun occasionally kicking off their perspex bubbles. And on the apron there are ten Chipmunks lined up, resplendent in rich scarlet red and brilliant white. It's the sort of day to appreciate how intrinsically beautiful flying can be. It's the sort of day when it's easy to understand why Fred and his instructors can't kick the habit.

Corporal Mark Hitch is fearful. He's drawn the short straw. His instructor is Peter Jennings, known as the hard man of the Chipmunk team, a reputation that has earned him the crew-room nickname 'Chopper'. But when they eventually meet, Mark is relieved to find that Mr Jennings seems a very cheerful axeman. He is in his late fifties, and has lost most of his hair but retained a youthful sparkle in his eyes and an infectious laugh. They head out to the apron, stopping to pick up their parachutes on the way. As they walk, Mark talks about the problems he had during the selection process. He managed to complete his thirteen hours Chipmunk flying, but never felt comfortable. 'It just didn't seem natural,' he confesses. He only scraped through selection as a borderline case – a 'training risk' in the jargon of the Corps – and he fears he will struggle to keep up. As Mark talks, Mr Jennings listens, trying to imagine how anyone can find flying 'unnatural'.

They get into their allotted plane – Mark at the front, Mr Jennings behind – and start the pre-flight drill. A groundcrewman from Bristows – the civilian company which has the Middle Wallop maintenance contract – arrives at the plane, checks the propeller and starts flooding the carburettor. For Mark the whole procedure is poignant: he has come on the course having done six years as a groundcrewman in the Army Air Corps. For six years he has been doing start-up checks for other pilots. Now he's in the cockpit and someone else is doing the checks for him: 'I often wondered, "Christ, why can't it be me in there? Why can't I have a go at that?"'

With a cough, a splutter and a deafening backfire the propeller kicks into life. Mark takes control and starts taxiing out to the runway. His career as an Army pilot begins here. But he can't help feeling apprehensive:

> It's going to be a hard year. You can get chopped at any stage. You can get chopped in week one or you can get chopped with only one week to go. It's always over you. You can never relax. For 365 days you're working until you get the wings on your chest.

Mark knows what failure means. Two days before the course began a friend of his was thrown off Course 353 – the course seven weeks ahead of 354. Like Mark, he was a groundcrewman who had been given the chance to become a pilot, but he

failed at the first hurdle. Now he's back on the ground again, with no prospect of ever making it as a pilot. In this game there are few second chances. Ironically, Mark has been allocated the same room in the corporals' block that his friend vacated: 'I'm stepping into dead men's shoes.' It hardly inspires confidence.

Nervously, Mark takes off and soars into the blue sky. 'Very good,' says Chopper, 'you might never have been away from it.' Mark's relief is tangible. They climb and climb, up to 5000 feet and level off. The South of England looks beautiful from this height. Mr Jennings points out the sights: 'Look there's Salisbury Cathedral at three o'clock.... Poole in the distance at one o'clock and over there at ten o'clock you can just see the Isle of Wight.' To his surprise, Mark is able to relax and admire the view. He carries out a steep turn to the left and heads in a south-westerly direction. He's still not convinced that there's anything 'natural' about leaning at 45 degrees, 5000 feet in the air, in a forty-year-old plane, but for the time being he's willing to give it the benefit of the doubt.

The next trainee to take off is Lieutenant Jenny Firth. Unsurprisingly, she makes a perfect ascent. It's unsurprising because she already has a private pilot's licence on fixed wing planes. She has been flying for eight years as a civilian, ever since a trip to the United States where she took her first lessons on the cheap (learning to fly is much more affordable in America than in Britain). Since then she has continued to fly just enough hours every year to maintain her licence. She's not sure what first made her want to fly. She thinks it goes back to her childhood, being brought up overseas and constantly flying back and forth to England. But now that she can fly, she is very clear what the buzz is:

> You're free. It's that feeling of being up in the air, with nothing underneath you. It's the extra plane, the third dimension, if you like. Everybody else is confined to the streets, walking around or in cars, but you're up there, going over traffic jams and flying around.

Jenny's experience has been in Cessna planes and the Chipmunk, with its old-fashioned joystick control, will be quite different. Nevertheless, she knows this phase will be more or less revision for her, and she starts with a definite

Flying is one part soaring through the skies and nine parts planning. Mark Hitch (right) and Jim LeCornu prepare for their next sortie.

Andy James, the man who would be Top Gun.

advantage over the others. She's not complaining – being the only woman among nine men will be hard enough.

The last in the air is Second Lieutenant Andy James. Like Mark, he has no previous flying experience, except the thirteen hours they all did on selection. But in his case selection was fully two years ago – he had to do an attachment in Northern Ireland before he could start the course – and he hasn't flown since then. He's now understandably nervous about getting back into a plane. He wonders how much he'll remember. 'People tell me it's like learning to ride a bike, and once up in the air it'll all come back to me. We'll see...'

He has been assigned Paul Miller as his instructor. He could not have chosen better. Mr Miller is a grown-up version of Andy: easy-going, wise-cracking and charming. Andy immediately warms to him: 'He's really mellow. Dead cool.' As it quickly becomes apparent that Andy can't remember the first thing about how to fly, Mr Miller has plenty of opportunities to demonstrate his mellowness.

'Whoa. Steady on. Full power. Climb now...' Mr Miller is coaxing Andy through a stall recovery. It's a straightforward manoeuvre, but one which requires precision handling, and Andy is struggling with his touch. 'What did you do wrong?' Mr Miller asks. Andy looks vacant. 'You whacked the stick forward in a brutal, licentious, soldierly-like way. Come on, none of this brutality.' Mr Miller tells him off, but he makes a joke of it at the same time. 'You've got to wait and push the stick forward when you feel the buffet, or *buffet* as the French say. Now try again.' Andy repeats the manoeuvre, but again loses control.

'What went wrong there?' Mr Miller asks.

'I was too brutal again, Sir?' Andy suggests speculatively.

'No, you weren't brutal enough that time.' Andy is starting to feel he can't win.

Before the end of the flight, Mr Miller pops the question: 'Have you ever seen the film *Top Gun*?' He knows full well that all trainees have seen *Top Gun* – most of them have watched it several times.

'Yes, Sir, I have.'

'Well I want you to be more like Tom Cruise, more punchy, more snappy. You look like Tom Cruise, now fly like him.'

Andy is delighted. His flight has been little short of a disaster – he can't remember how to read the compass, how to carry out safety drills, how to hold a heading. But all these things pale into insignificance now he's been paid the ultimate compliment, comparison with Tom Cruise in *Top Gun*.

For most trainee pilots – and Andy James is no exception – Hollywood's flying movies are a source of inspiration. What they know about the excitement and allure of flying they've learned from films like *Blue Thunder*, *Apocalypse Now*, *Wings of the Apache* and *The Right Stuff*. But number one in the feel-good wanna-fly stakes is still *Top Gun*. They love Tom Cruise's cool, his confidence, his aviator shades. They love the way he wins over the beautiful instructor. But most of all they love the flying scenes – F14 jets breaking the sound barrier, soaring high into the stratosphere, diving low, doing stunts. Military flying – Hollywood-style – has the power to take your breath away. Small wonder that thousands of young men – and now a few young women – want to follow in Tom Cruise's footsteps.

Back on the ground, ten new pilots have finished flying and are sharing stories in their crewroom. The talk is of loop-the-loops, wingovers and barrel rolls. Mark Hitch is particularly elated. His flight has been such a relief. Nothing went wrong. Mr Jennings never lost his cool, he even complimented Mark on his final landing. All the flights they do on the course are assessed and colour-coded: blue for excellent; green for average; brown for below average; and red for fail. Mark has been scored green for today's sortie.

Andy is quieter. He has scored a brown, bordering on red. He prefers to cast a veil over the flying and talk about his likeness to Tom Cruise. In fact Andy looks nothing like Tom Cruise. If anything, he most resembles Hugh Laurie playing Bertie Wooster – the same wide-eyed innocence and Home Counties accent. Nor does his antique Chipmunk look anything like an F14. But it doesn't stop him dreaming. The reality may be *Biggles*, but the dream is all *Top Gun*. 'I just want to be one of those strut-around fancy pilots. It'll be so cool.'

As the sun drops behind the hangar, the trainees make their way back to their quarters. The first day of flying is over.

Monday, 14 March

Course 354 are given just five flying hours in which to go solo – five hours to learn how to take off, fly a circuit of the airfield and land again safely, on their own. Fred Trowern explains the rationale: 'You had thirteen hours experience on selection, we give you another five here – that makes eighteen. In eighteen hours anyone should be able to go solo. If my mother was still alive, I could probably get her solo in eighteen hours.' The trainees look unconvinced. Five hours seems like a very short time.

The weather doesn't help. In good conditions they could fly the five hours on consecutive days (the trainees are limited to one hour-long sortie a day). But this is March and the weather has been foul. At this stage of the training, they aren't allowed to fly when the wind is above 15 knots, or the cloud base is below 2000 feet. Consequently there was very little flying in the first week and they are getting restless. If they do manage to grab a clear hour's flying, they then find themselves waiting several days before the next hour, by which time they've forgotten what they've learnt. It's impossible to get any continuity.

When the course are grounded, they spend the day in the classroom, attending lectures and briefings. They are starting to realize just how much technical detail there is to learn: meteorology, navigation, principles of flight, and so on. Flying is one part soaring through the skies and nine parts planning. The only respite from the workload comes by way of occasional instructor anecdotes. One of the instructors in particular, Mr Scott who teaches principles of flight, spends a fair percentage of each lesson telling stories of his flying career. Like any group

The first challenge: five hours to go solo in a Chipmunk...

of pupils sensing a point of weakness in their teacher, the course wind him up remorselessly: 'Sir, remind us what happened to you that time in Burma?' They know the resulting tale will occupy the rest of the lesson.

Today is the day of their first exam – a test on all the safety drills required to fly solo. It is supervised by Fred who takes it very seriously: 'Thirty-three straightforward questions – you should know all the answers, but I'm a generous man and I've made the passmark 90 per cent.' The trainees chew their pens and fill in their test papers. It's all too reminiscent of school days.

Because there are officers and non-commissioned officers on the same course, the educational background of the group varies greatly. The three officers stayed on at school for the sixth form, they took their A-levels and one of them – JP Miller – went on to university and got a degree. The seven NCOs, on the other hand, all left school at sixteen and managed only a handful of GCSE passes between them. For them, the academic side of the course is as daunting – if not more so – than the flying. Mark Hitch's story is typical: he was so keen to join the Army he didn't bother to sit any exams at school. He now knows he'll have to work harder than the rest just to keep up with all the technical detail.

In fact nearly all the corporals get respectable results in Fred's test and score better than the 90 per cent pass mark. True to form, the only two people to manage 100 per cent – Jenny and JP – are both officers. But the real surprise of the group is Andy who fails the test with just 84 per cent. Fred is unimpressed: 'The lad's not stupid, he's just lazy. He obviously hasn't put the work in. But don't worry,' he says with some menace, 'we'll sort him out before we're through with him.'

Andy gets a 'beasting' from Mr Miller. 'You'll have to do a re-sit now, and if you don't pass that you'll be packing your bags.' Andy looks duly shamefaced.

At 4.30 p.m. the day ends. The trainees leave their crewroom in Hangar Three, mount their bikes and go their separate ways. The corporals head for the cookhouse where the evening meal is served straight away. They have to rush because the last meal is served at 5.15 p.m. The cookhouse is a huge self-service canteen capable of feeding 250 soldiers at a time. The food is strictly school dinners – chips or custard with everything. And the ambience is strictly squaddie – conversations about girls, pubs and favourite TV shows. Corporals Hitch, Lock and LeCornu can recite verbatim sequences from all four series of *Blackadder*. They keep up long conversations in character, which are hilarious to the three of them, but unfathomable to anyone else. Often the repartee continues long after they've left the cookhouse and returned to their rooms.

Evenings in the officers' mess are very different. The normal routine runs like this: 5–6 p.m., tea and toast are served in the anteroom; 6–7 p.m., officers retire to their rooms to dress for the evening (dark suits are compulsory every evening except Wednesdays, when a jacket and tie are acceptable); 7–7.30 p.m., a quick drink in the bar; 7.30–8.30 p.m., supper is served. It's a silver service affair: wine, waiters, and menus printed in French. Chandeliers hang from the ceiling, and on the wall there is a full-length portrait of the Queen. The food itself is nothing very special – not much better than the corporals' fare –

but that's not the point. The setting, the rules, the formality – they're all designed to remind these young men that they're special, they're an elite.

Andy James is tucking into his chicken à l'orange. The troubles of today's test seem to be forgotten. 'It's just a temporary blip. I'll work harder next time and I'll be fine.' He's more interested in chatting to the other officers on his table about plans for a party at the weekend. He loves mess life. He loves the security, the ease, the camaraderie:

> It's just like public school, but here we get paid as well. The majority of us are fairly young and we're all on pilot's courses, so we can talk about how things are going in the evening. ... I don't mind at all having to dress up in suits and things, because it's carrying on tradition. You know, we're meant to behave like officers and gentlemen.

The waiter brings him his crème caramel.

In his room in Hotspur House – the block for single corporals – Mark Hitch is munching his way through some Pot Noodles. 'The trouble is, we eat so early I get hungry again by nine o'clock.' He's half-browsing through his flying manual, half-watching *Red Dwarf* on the television. Does he resent the treatment the officers get? 'No, it's just the way things are. They eat their way, we eat ours. That's the Army way. Anyway, I wouldn't want to wear a suit for mealtimes. I'm quite happy in a jumper and jeans.' It transpires that the only time Mark has ever been in an officers' mess is to serve food at a function.

Jenny Firth avoids the officer-ranks divide to some extent. Because she is married, she's entitled to a house on the married patch, rather than a room in the officers' mess. She likes the freedom and normality it affords: 'I can come home in the evenings, put on any old clothes and make myself something to eat, in my own time.' She's happy to turn up to the mess for any functions, but otherwise she gives it a wide berth, leaving it to the likes of Andy and his friends. Of all the trainees, she enjoys the closest thing to an ordinary domestic life away fromthe course. But even she is touched by the relative privilege of the system: her house as an officer is far larger and better appointed than anything a married NCO would receive. And for the next few months her husband Steve – a lieutenant in the

Paras – is stationed up near Birmingham, so she has the place all to herself.

To an outsider it seems strange that a group of trainees on the same course, receiving the same tuition, are treated equally until 4.30 p.m. and then so differently afterwards. But to those inside the system – officers *and* corporals – the division is embraced as perfectly natural. On duty, they're a team. Off duty, it's each to their own, and ne'er shall the twain meet. It's the way things have always been done and always will be done, and it goes some way to explain the fundamental stability of the Army, at a time when nearly every other major British institution faces a crisis of confidence.

Wednesday, 16 March

At last the weather has relented. Middle Wallop has been promised two days of clear skies and low winds. The stop-go flying programme is definitely in go mode again. Fred is trying to get everyone solo within these two days. Suddenly, after a week and a half of inactivity, the circuit above the airfield is buzzing with Chipmunks. For now, all fancy manoeuvres are forgotten; the trainees are concentrating only on their circuit flying.

Take off. Safety checks at 200 feet. Climb to 800 feet. Turn left on to crosswind leg. Hold 90 knots. Turn on to downwind leg. Remember to do safety checks. Check heading. Turn on to base leg. Select a landing slot. Turn on to finals. Change attitude of plane. Descend, cut speed to 60 knots. Never go below 60. Level off. Aim to hit the ground with all three wheels at the same time. Land. Make sure the plane is down safely. Then take off and start again. A circuit takes about six minutes. To fly one after another is a test of precision and concentration.

As expected, the first to make it solo is Jenny Firth. It may not be a surprise, but it's still a thrill to cross the solo barrier in a new aircraft:

> It's a wonderful feeling. Your instructor decides you're up to it and you might be able to get the Chipmunk back on the ground again. He gives you the thumbs up and waves you off. And in some ways it takes a lot of pressure off flying by yourself, because you haven't

> got somebody sitting in the back watching what all the dials are doing. And it's very nice actually making it down without doing a great deal of damage.

Jenny knows that her early advantage will run out once the Chipmunk phase is over and the course start flying helicopters. Then she will be on an equal footing with the rest of them. But, for now, she is grateful for her previous experience. It has helped her win the initial respect of the other trainees and instructors. They know they're dealing with a serious pilot, someone with proven potential.

Looking ahead, Jenny is less worried about the flying than about the military aspects of the course. So far, her Army career has been spent in offices, a long way from the frontline. She admits to being 'very ignorant' of tactics, and the latter part of the course is all about tactics. For now, Jenny is cruising, but she is intelligent enough to know that things are going to get much harder as the year progresses.

Against the odds, Andy James also manages to go solo within the five-hour limit. After the problems he had with his first flight and first exam, it looked an evens bet that he would fall at the first hurdle. But appearances can be deceptive. Andy's nonchalance hides a strong desire to succeed and, more importantly, an expectation of success. He is well practised in the art of doing just enough to get by. He thinks it is crass to be seen trying too hard – he just pulls out the stops when it matters. It is a philosophy that got him through public school and Sandhurst, and now it has got him solo in a Chipmunk.

For the first time in his life, Andy is flying an aircraft on his own. He's 800 feet above Middle Wallop in control:

> I'm sitting there thinking, oh my God, he's not here! But, to be honest, I'm concentrating so much on getting it right that I'm pretending Mr Miller is there and I'm sort of telling myself off as I'm going around. And I suddenly realize that, you know, I've got it right and I'm actually holding the aircraft in the right attitude and I'm doing everything properly.

His instructor is not convinced. Mr Miller has allowed Andy to go solo but, as he watches the circuit from the mobile observation booth beside the runway, he admits to having doubts about

The hardest thing about flying a Chipmunk is landing it.

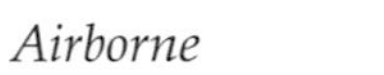

Andy's prospects: 'On his last three circuits he came good and did some reasonable landings. But he's still a bit rough and he'll have to get a lot better if he's going to pass the course.'

In the air, Andy starts his final approach. His speed drops off and he has to remind himself to stay at 70 knots. It seems to confirm Mr Miller's view: 'He can do it, but he just keeps forgetting things, all sorts of normal things. I don't know why it is... perhaps he hasn't got the right temperament.' Andy lands, all three wheels touching down at the same time. Mr Miller smiles: 'That was the best landing he's done all day... for which I'm truly grateful!'

Back in the hangar, Mr Miller and Andy carry out a simple but significant ritual. After finishing the paperwork that follows each sortie, the instructor hands the trainee a log book. It is a small hardback book with a lot of lines and columns. It looks much like an accountant's ledger. But with this small book Andy has symbolically moved from the massed ranks of wannabes to the select club of solo pilots. With this book, he is deemed to have a flying career ahead of him worth logging. Mr Miller shakes his hand and welcomes him to the club. Andy looks chuffed.

In another corner of the hangar, a less happy ritual is being played out. Mark Hitch has flown his fifth hour and failed to go solo. Mr Jennings, his instructor, has scored the flight a red and is now debriefing him. The progress he showed on his first flight has not been matched by his circuit work. His biggest problem is landing: either he keeps the stick too far back and never finds the ground; or he pushes it too far forward and bounces. Until he can land safely and consistently he will not be allowed to go solo. And now he has simply run out of time – his five hours are up.

A disappointed Mark Hitch shuffles into Fred Trowern's office. He hears confirmation of the bad news: 'We've decided to place you on review.' But Fred tries to put a gloss on the situation. 'Think of it as three extra flying hours we're going to give you, free of charge.' This is the review equation: Mark will have three more hours with a new instructor in which to achieve solo standard. If, at the end of the three hours, he makes it solo he will continue with his training as if nothing has happened. But if he still can't go solo he'll be chopped from the course. Fred puts it in his own inimitable way: 'At that point we'll have to say "I'm sorry Horst, for you the war is over"(delivered in best World War Two accent).'

It is the end of the flying day and Mark returns to his room, reeling. He came on the course to fly helicopters, but if he can't sort things out fast he won't even see day one of rotary training. He'll be just another aspiring helicopter pilot, defeated by fixed wing flying. He remembers his friend who was chopped on the Chipmunk phase; is he going to go the same way? He treks out to the public phone box and rings his parents in Penrith. When he tells his mother he's on review, she congratulates him. He has to put her right. 'No, you don't understand, Mum. It means I'm doing crap.'

At the officers' mess the drinks are on Andy. There is a tradition in the mess that whenever anyone passes a significant hurdle on their training, they 'ring the bell' – a brass handbell, standing innocuously on the bar next to a small garden gnome. Once the bell is rung, mayhem ensues. Everybody in earshot is entitled to get a drink from the ringer. The secret is in the timing. The crafty – or poor – choose to ring the bell at moments when they know the mess is quiet, and the resulting damage to their mess bill is limited. The extravagant – or foolhardy – wait until just before supper is served when the mess is at its busiest, and make an occasion of it. Needless to say, Andy takes the latter option: 'My mess bill's going to be enormous but, what the hell, it's got to be done.' The consensus of the other officers in the bar is that Andy is definitely a 'good egg'.

Thursday, 17 March

Mark takes off on the first of his three review flights. His new instructor is Ian Hamilton, a less formidable proposition than Mr Jennings. Mark is glad of the change; he didn't get on with Chopper. Things started out fine but, as the pressure of circuit flying mounted, the relationship between them deteriorated. Jennings thought Hitch was a bit of a wimp: 'After one sortie he told me he wasn't enjoying it and that made me wonder whether he really wants it hard enough, or whether he's just playing at it.' Hitch thought Jennings was a bit of a bully: 'If I was slow doing a turn or something he'd tell me off for daydreaming. And that would knock my confidence. I don't like being bawled at when I haven't done anything wrong.' Whatever the truth of the matter, Mark's flying suffered and Mr Hamilton now faces a dual task: not only to improve Mark's handling skills, but also to rebuild his confidence.

Mr Hamilton has the air of a prep school housemaster about him: paternalistic, kind-hearted, but a little pedantic. It's not a style that seems conducive to Mark's dry northern humour, but it works. From the start, Mark feels in gentler hands and he's able to relax more. His landings are still a problem, but at least he can see a way forward. Midway through the sortie, Mr Hamilton asks Mark how he's feeling:

'Er, a bit more relaxed. I've got a bit more confidence back.'

'Good.'

'But I'm still being a bit slow to make decisions.'

'Close to the ground I'd agree with that. Aggressive decision-making close to the ground has got to be coming from you. You can't afford to be too analytical.'

The rest of the course are feeling the shock of having someone on review. Until now they could have been forgiven for thinking they were at a flying club, and being paid to lark about in the sky. But suddenly it's serious: only a month into the course and already the first of them is facing the chop. Superficially, they are confident he'll pass and all will be fine. But they don't really know what to expect. It is hard for them to gauge how badly Mark is actually doing. On the face of it, he seems no worse than the rest of them. So, if he's in trouble now, who'll be next? This is the most unsettling aspect of someone going on review. It reminds the others of their own vulnerability.

They are in the gym, playing basketball, but their thoughts are with Mark up in the air. As Andy James puts it: 'When it gets to this stage it's frightening. He's under so much pressure. We try and cheer him up, but in the end it's up to him. We can't fly it for him.' On the exterior wall of the gym, above the door, hangs a sign: 'Winners Never Quit, Quitters Never Win'. It is a well-known military epigram, but it seems particularly apt at this moment.

The person at the eye of the storm is remaining remarkably calm, at least outwardly. Mark is in no mood to quit, but neither is he setting great store by what happens. 'If I pass, I pass. If not, I go back to my old job. It's not the end of the world. They can't make me pregnant or anything.' It is hard to know how much of this is bluff – Mark is a squaddie, and squaddies know how to bury their emotions. But real or not, his come-what-may attitude is helping him cope with the pressure. Rather than hide away, he invites the rest of the course – officers and all – over to his room in the evening for a revision session ahead of tomorrow's exam.

In the event, everyone turns up with books and beer in hand, but not a lot of revising is done. They seem more interested in taking the mickey out of Andy James, who has come straight from the mess in his suit and tie. It is as if Andy doesn't quite understand the dress code of Hotspur House. It is his first visit – and turns out to be his last. For the rest of the year, none of the officers are invited back to Hotspur House. Future social gatherings will happen on 'neutral' territory.

Mark goes through the motions of revising. But, however important the exams are made out to be, he knows he won't get thrown off the course for poor exam results. The only test that really matters is in the air. He's waiting to prove himself.

Tuesday, 22 March

It's 8 a.m. and it is wet and windy, too wet and windy for the rest of the course to fly. However, Fred and Mr Hamilton have decided that today is to be the day of Mark's third and final review flight. The Meteorological Office have promised a possible 'window' at 10 o'clock, when the wind will drop enough for Mark to fly. This is to be make-or-break day for him: 'The next flight will determine the rest of my flying career. Pass it and I carry on. Fail it and I stay on the ground. It's got to be perfect... perfect.' Mark stands in the door of the crewroom, looking out over the airfield to the grey skies beyond. He seems oblivious of the other people in the room. In training jargon, he's getting focused.

At 9.30 a.m. he starts his pre-flight routine at the plane. Check canopy, wings and wheels. Inspect engine for any signs of leakage. Meanwhile his instructor, Mr Hamilton, is waiting in the instructors' crewroom. 'This is a very important flight for him – he must go solo today. But I'm optimistic. He's shown progress over the last couple of flights and if he keeps up the same rate of progress he *should* be all right.'

Mark gets into the Chipmunk and starts checking the internal controls. By now the routine is instinctive – check pitot head, engine temperature and pressure, fuel contents – but suddenly it's broken by Mr Hamilton. Normally he only arrives at the plane once all the checks are over, but this time he has come early, to bring bad news.

'I'm sorry Mark, the wind's got up again. We can't fly at the moment. We're waiting for the Met to tell us what's going to happen for the rest of the day.'

'Don't worry, Sir. I can wait.'

'Good lad. I'm really sorry about this.' Mr Hamilton seems more upset by the delay than Mark.

Back in the crewroom and another cup of tea. Mark's gaze is fixed on the fluorescent orange windsock. As a rule of thumb, you can tell the wind speed from the angle of the windsock – anything greater than 45 degrees and the wind is out of limits, anything less and it's flyable. At the moment it's standing at about 60 degrees. Mark can't decide what would be better now – for the wind to stay high all day and for the flight to be postponed in the hope of better weather tomorrow. Or for the wind to drop, so he can fly today and resolve the uncertainty sooner rather than later.

By eleven o'clock a decision has been made for him. Imperceptibly at first, the wind has started dropping and the angle of the windsock is now definitely below 45 degrees. The Met Office have revised their forecast again and are predicting that the wind will stay below 15 knots for the next two hours. Then it will start gusting badly as another frontal system arrives. Mark is told to take off as soon as possible. He returns to his aircraft, carries out all the same checks and starts the engine. Mr Hamilton joins him. The groundcrewman removes the chocks. He taxis out to the runway and takes off. This is it – an hour to fly better than he's ever flown before. The others have told Mark the formula: three good circuits and three good landings, and the instructor will get out and let him go solo.

Thirty seconds into the flight, Mark completes his after take-off checks and his instructor gives him immediate feedback: 'OK, good start. Perhaps slightly more nose down would make me feel more comfortable, but you got airborne at around the right speed.' As Mark listens to his instructor he loses his concentration for a moment and the Chipmunk loses height suddenly. 'Whoa... keep that lookout going. Don't ever take your attention off the horizon.'

First landing – a wobble and a bump, but not too bad. Second landing – all three wheels touch down at the same time, perfection. Mark is even complimented on it: 'Good one. You're seeing the ground well this morning.' Third landing – a couple of bounces, but Mark recovers it in time. He waits to hear the verdict, but Mr Hamilton just asks him to carry on and do another circuit. What does that mean? Weren't his landings good enough? Or is Mr Hamilton just being extra cautious? It annoys Mark that the instructor sits behind the trainee in a Chipmunk, so he can't see the expression on his face. Is he smiling or not? He's barely uttered twenty words since the start of the flight. Is that good or bad? Mark nervously flies a fourth circuit and makes an adequate, but by no means perfect, landing. Again he waits to hear Mr Hamilton's verdict.

'Right, pull into a stop. I didn't let you know what was going on there, because I didn't want it to condition the way you flew that last circuit. You know why, don't you?'

'No, Sir.'

'I'm getting out and I'm going to let you go solo. Is that OK with you?'

'Er, yes, Sir.' A very broad smile is creeping across Mark's face.

'You've done well. There are no ifs or buts. You're really ready for it.'

With fifteen minutes left on the clock, Mr Hamilton has finally decided Mark has reached solo standard. He opens the canopy and gets out. 'See you in six minutes. Try and enjoy yourself.' Mr Hamilton walks away to the mobile observation booth, leaving Mark in the Chipmunk – alone. Once again he goes through the take-off drill: 'Trims are two divisions nose down, engine temperature and pressure are within limits. Harness is locked and tight. Hood is forward and locked.... *I have control!*' He savours those last three words.

Just as he's about to engage throttle and take off, the radio crackles into life. 'Middle Wallop Tower here with a message from Met – the wind is now 20 knots, gusting 27.' Mark's smile immediately disappears. The wind has crept up over the limit again. What does he do now? He looks over at the observation booth to see if his instructor has heard the same message, but gets no reaction. He rationalizes that the weather warning was a general one, and that he himself has received no direct order to abort the flight. If he's ever going to go solo, now is surely the moment. He decides not to hang around to await further clarification.

Full throttle. Speed up to 50 knots. Nose up, and away. 'Airborne!' Mark shouts out to himself. His elation and relief are overwhelming. The look on his face gives the lie to his previous show of indifference. He's wanted this moment so badly. Everything has changed – his body language, his mood, his confidence. He's flying on adrenaline, delivering a cod commentary as he goes: 'And the crowd went wild...'

Of all the circuits he has done, none has seemed so much fun or gone so quickly. At one moment he's muttering 'looking good, looking good', the next he's having to remind himself to start his final approach: 'Right, let's get this baby on the ground...'

Mark knows that this is the final test. If he's to come off review and prove himself worthy as a solo pilot, then he'll have to show he really can land accurately and safely on his own. As he loses height and heads for the ground, Mr Hamilton is watching him closely from the observation booth. It is a nerve-racking moment for him as well; this is when his judgement is put to the test. He has made the decision to allow Mark to fly on his own. He also knows that the wind is over limits and by rights Mark shouldn't be flying. If anything goes wrong, he'll bear responsibility.

In the event, Mark lands safely. It is not his best landing of the day – he bounces a couple of times down the runway – but instructor and trainee are happy enough. Mark even allows himself a self-satisfied laugh as he realizes he's down safely: 'Hee, hee, hee.' He taxis back to the start point where Mr Hamilton is waiting to congratulate him. Normally they would now carry on, fly another dual circuit and then Mark would do a couple more solo circuits. But, given the wind, Mr Hamilton tells Mark they've been called back in. Mark will have to content himself with six minutes of solo flying – at least for now. Six minutes or six hours, he doesn't care. He's now a solo pilot and, more importantly, he's off review.

Back in the crewroom, he's barely able to contain himself: 'I'm chuffed as fucking bananas... Brilliant... mega!' One by one, the others shake his hand and make a fuss of him. Their relief is twofold: they're glad for him, but they're also reassured for themselves. They've seen that it is possible to go on review – to reach the brink – and still survive. They need not view the prospect of review with quite the same trepidation.

Mark spends the rest of the afternoon coming down from the high. He's also able to reflect on what he's been through. 'I've seen what pressure is all about. I found myself snapping at people, getting pissed off quickly. Normally, I'm quite easy-going. But I could feel my character changing.' He knows he's not out of the

The Hollywood Course relax. They have all made it through the Chipmunk phase, now they can look forward to flying helicopters.

woods yet. He's got to catch up on the work he's missed while being on review. He also knows that the long-term omens are not good for him, having struggled at the first pressure point. But on the plus side, he can feel his confidence returning, like blood pumping freely through his veins again. He feels ready to tackle whatever challenges lie ahead.

For the first time he understands why people talk of flying as a drug. Previously, he'd denied any great love for flying: 'It's just a job'. Now he's willing to admit that maybe, just maybe, 'It could grow on me!'

Friday, 29 April

The ten members of Course 354 have taken their final Chipmunk handling tests – all ten have passed, and have achieved an acceptable standard as fixed wing pilots. It's not been easy, but they've managed it without casualty. They can now look forward to starting rotary training.

After going solo, Mark's flying improved markedly. He was able to catch up with the rest of the course and complete the training schedule without further difficulties. His end-of-term report from Mr Hamilton was largely positive:

> He reached a good standard after a poor start caused largely by a lack of confidence. His confidence is still fragile and needs bolstering a little while longer. Strong potential, as he is a hard worker with a good level of all-round ability.

Of the rest of the trainees, Jenny and two others with previous fixed wing experience – Corporal Mickey Rooney and Lieutenant JP Miller – topped the class. Everyone else scored an average pass. But they are all quick to play down the significance of the results. Those who have done well claim that – fate being what it is – they'll probably be the first to come unstuck in rotary training. Those who have done poorly claim that Fixed Wing proves nothing; the only thing that matters is how well they fly a helicopter.

It is certainly true that helicopters and planes are very different and many good fixed wing pilots never master helicopters, and vice versa. But they shouldn't dismiss the fixed wing results too easily. If nothing else, some patterns have been established. And patterns established so early have a habit of repeating themselves as a course progresses. If a pilot has a problem with attitude or awareness at this stage, the chances are that the problem will resurface throughout the course.

But this is no time for gloomy thoughts about future difficulties. For now, the course are in a mood for celebration. And they're celebrating, as every course before them has, with a team photograph taken next to a Chipmunk. But being a special course – 'the Hollywood course' – something more creative is expected of them than a run-of-the-mill snap, so they've got themselves dressed up for the occasion in antique flying gear, borrowed from the Middle Wallop Museum. The look is a bit mixed up – part *Biggles,* part *Dambusters* – but the total effect is very much of some golden age. Here they stand, ten flying aces ready to tackle Gerry. It all seems a long way from dreams of *Top Gun*.

Chapter Two

The Rotary Club

Tuesday, 10 May

Middle Wallop, Hampshire

The carrot is still dangling, tantalizingly out of reach. Course 354 have finished two and a half months of fixed wing training, and they're desperate to start flying helicopters. But they'll have to wait a bit longer. For the time being, all training has stopped. There are more pressing concerns.

This is the day of the Guidon Parade, the day the Army Air Corps wins its colours. Prince Charles is coming to Middle Wallop, and they are putting on a party. Yesterday the marquees arrived, along with a temporary grandstand and a shiny new VIPs' enclosure. Today everything is ready. Middle Wallop has been transformed from busy airfield to royal circus.

Prince Charles is the new Colonel-in-Chief of the Corps. He's coming to present them with their regimental standard – their guidon – in recognition of the teeth-arm role the Corps played in the Falklands and, more recently, the Gulf. Only regiments such as the Cavalry and Infantry, which engage directly with the enemy, are awarded Guidons, and for the Army Air Corps to achieve this recognition is evidence that a young corps has come of age. As Major General Simon Lyttle, Director of the Corps, puts it: 'In Army terms we're rather *parvenu*. Some other regiments are celebrating their tercentenaries, whereas we have a history stretching back no more than thirty-seven years. So it's a great honour for us to receive this award.'

The Corps is marking the occasion with the most elaborate helicopter parade ever staged in Britain: forty helicopters flying in formation carrying 400 men on to the Middle Wallop airfield. It is a major feat of co-ordination that has taken months of planning and days of rehearsal. It has been designed to run with split-second accuracy.

At 11.00 a.m. precisely, Prince Charles's helicopter lands. It's a standard Army helicopter fitted with a new carpet and a first-class airliner seat. He makes his way to a ceremonial dais situated on the airfield where Runway 20 would normally be. He takes his seat on the dais alongside the Director and Colonel Commandant of the Corps. The regimental band are playing 'God Save the Queen' to welcome him. A crowd of pilots, past and present, are watching from the grandstand and enclosure behind the dais. Everyone is waiting for something to happen.

Half a mile from the airfield, in the playing field beside the officers' mess, things *are* happening. Forty Lynx helicopters are parked in eight neat rows of five. At precisely 11.05 a.m. all forty of them come to life with one breath. Forty rotor blades start at exactly the same moment. Forty landing lights strobe. Forty tonnes of downwash pound the grass.

At 11.07 a.m the first five Lynx take off together. They pause for a moment, pick up speed and fly out in a line over the officers' mess. Rather than take a direct route to the airfield, they make a low-level detour by way of Knock Wood, taking care to stay below the skyline at all times. Thirty seconds later the next wave of five takes off and flies the same path, followed thirty seconds later by another, and another, and another.

By 11.09 a.m. the crowd at the airfield are on the point of growing restless. Nothing seems to be happening. Prince Charles politely enquires of his hosts whether everything is in order. But then, from the middle distance behind Knock Wood, they appear – five helicopters turning on their final approach. The Lynx is a large, wide-bodied, powerful helicopter. Five of them moving together dominate the skyline. All five of them descend to a point 50 yards from the dais. As soon as skids touch down, thirty troops jump out, and assemble in parade formation. The troops are Army Air Corps soldiers – ground crewmen, air troopers and gunners from regiments around the world. They are dressed in formal service dress, each one carrying a rifle in one hand and light blue beret in the other. Once the helicopters have dropped off their passengers, they take off and scurry away, revealing the second wave behind them.

For the next twelve minutes, wave after wave of helicopters land, disgorging more troops. By the end, 400 soldiers are lined up on parade in front of the dais. At a command from the Regimental Sergeant Major, all 400 put their berets on and stand to attention. One last helicopter lands and out marches the colour party, in full ceremonial dress. At the head of the group is Lieutenant Will Fanshawe, a young officer from Pilot's Course 348. He has been given the honour of carrying the guidon, which he places on a drumhead – a makeshift altar made up of a couple of bass drums.

Prince Charles and the Army Air Corps dignitaries make their way out to the guidon. Before it can be officially handed over to the Corps it needs to be blessed. The Chaplain General of the Army does the honours:

> We stand before God this day to ask His blessing on this guidon, and to pray that it may be a residing symbol of our resolve to preserve and sustain the great traditions of bravery and self-sacrifice of which we are the proud inheritors. Let us pray.

Lieutenant Fanshawe now lowers himself on to one knee, and Prince Charles gives him the guidon. It is an elegant maroon flag with the Corps emblem – an eagle – carefully embroidered at its centre. The words, 'Falklands 1982' and 'The Gulf 1991' flank the eagle. With a salute, Prince Charles completes the ceremony and returns to his place on the dais, from where he watches the guidon being paraded through the troops. The band strikes up the Corps regimental march 'Recce Flight'. It is a combination – music, guidon, royalty – that causes a few moist eyes among the veteran pilots who are in the audience.

The members of Course 354 are watching. The officers, Andy James, Jenny Firth and JP Miller, are on VIP escort duty. Two of the corporals, Mickey Rooney and Nigel Harrison, are in the guard party at the dais. The rest are among the spectators. They are all impressed, especially with the formation flying. But they find it hard to get emotional. At this stage they are more interested in becoming pilots than part of the Corps. That identification will come only when they've

Prince Charles hands over the guidon, and symbolically the Army Air Corps has come of age.

AAC

This is the most ambitious helicopter parade ever attempted in Britain.

passed the course and spent some time in operational squadrons.

To put it bluntly, the trainees on Course 354 still feel like outsiders, and this is very much an event for insiders. To the outsider, it is a mystery that so much time, effort and money can be devoted to the unveiling of a flag. But to the insider, such considerations are redundant. This is tradition; this is the Army Air Corps making its mark on military history.

The parade ends with a fly-past, involving all the aircraft at Middle Wallop: the Lynx, Gazelles, Chipmunks and an assortment of antique military planes and helicopters. It is an extraordinary sight: sixty aircraft flying in tight formation. It is also a cue for luncheon to commence.

Prince Charles makes his way into the marquee, shakes hands with the VIP guests, and joins the senior officers for a meal. Beforehand, his staff have ensured that the caterers are supplied with his special silver cutlery. The Prince only ever eats with his own knife and fork. In the entrance to the marquee, Andy James is on cloakroom duty. He has been charged with the task of looking after the Prince's sword and beret.

After a light lunch Prince Charles leaves with his two hosts, the Director and the Colonel Commandant. Andy hands them their swords and head-dresses. Unfortunately he gets the berets of the Prince and the Colonel Commandant confused and, with great comic timing, the two men put them on at the same time, only to realize they don't fit. They laugh and swap them over, while Andy goes red with embarrassment and quietly wishes the ground would open up and swallow him.

Soon after, the royal helicopter picks up the Colonel-in-Chief and whisks him away: away from this simple world of parades, Guidons and berets, back to a harsher world of tabloid revelations and speculation about the future of the royal family.

Once the guest of honour has left, the members of the Corps can relax. The senior officers carry on dining and much wine flows. The others enjoy themselves in the beer tent. For the Regimental Sergeant Major, who was charged with organizing the event, there's an overwhelming sense of relief at a job well done: 'It's been a good day... fantastic. The padres have worked hard to guarantee good weather, the soldiers have all done well and I'm bloody glad it's over!'

For others the work continues. No sooner is the Guidon Parade over than Middle Wallop has to prepare itself for its biennial International Air Show. Starting tomorrow, for the next five days, there will be a trade fair, a flying competition, a technical symposium and two open days at the weekend where the public will be treated to a flying display, the Radio One Roadshow and a guest appearance from Mr Blobby. For Course 354 it means five more quiet days with all normal flying suspended. They'll have to while away the time helping out in the information tent, or in the car park, or as markers in the helicopter competition. Such is the lot of a junior trainee.

The Air Show has its compensations however. The trade fair attracts some of the latest helicopter hardware from around the world, and for Course 354 it is a chance to find out what the next generation of military flying involves. They'll get to see the different attack helicopters vying for the Army Air Corps' approval. It is an enormous contract – two billion pounds worth of attack helicopter, the largest defence procurement ever made in peacetime – so it's not surprising that the manufacturers are using this opportunity to show off their wares.

Less than an hour after the Guidon Parade ends, the first of the attack helicopters arrives in advance of the Air Show. It is an Apache – the American star of the Gulf War. Matt-black, ugly and threatening, it bears more than a passing resemblance to a praying mantis. The contrast with the Lynx – the Army Air Corps' only existing armed helicopter – couldn't be greater. The Apache is designed more like a fighter plane than a traditional helicopter. Its two seats are set in separate cockpits in tandem, one behind the other, so the fuselage can be kept as narrow as possible, presenting the smallest target to the enemy. Where the missiles on the Lynx were added as an afterthought, the automatic cannon and Hellfire missiles are fully integrated into the design of the Apache, operated on the nod of a pilot's helmet by virtual reality technology inside the cockpit. It is a purpose-built killing machine, offering 'total lethality' in the words of its promotional brochure.

A small group watches in awe as the Apache – on loan from the US Army in Germany – shuts down, and the two American pilots make their appearance, chewing gum and sporting aviator shades. They look every inch like extras from *Top Gun*. Andy James and his friend Gavin from Course 353 are the first to step forward and take a close look at the helicopter. To their delight they are allowed to sit in the cockpits: Andy at the back; Gavin at the front. They are like two excited kids playing with a new toy.

'Oh God, I'd love to fly this. It's sex! ' Andy enthuses.

'Yeah, imagine going down the pub in this. Hey girls wanna come outside and see my chopper?' Gavin laughs at the wonder of his fantasy.

'I've never seen so many buttons and management systems in all my life. It's awesome.... Mind you, I'll be all right. Flick this switch and we're away. OK Gav, you have control.'

'I have control. Where's the ignition key?... And where do you put your beer? There's nowhere to put your beer!'

It is certainly a sobering thought – frightening perhaps – that these two lads, still so naive, could really be flying an attack helicopter within the next few years. But it is a reality for everyone on Course 354. They know that the best of them will go on to form the first cohort of twenty-first century attack pilots. Seeing the Apache close up, this prospect suddenly becomes more meaningful. It is an incentive – if incentive were needed – to redouble their efforts on the course. Today they have seen their future.

Monday, 16 May

Seafield Park, Hampshire

The Guidon Parade and Air Show are over, but Course 354 still can't start the Basic Rotary phase of their training. They face one more hurdle, a week of aero-medical and survival training. Before they can make their first flights, they have to understand the physiological effects of flying in a helicopter, and they need to know how to react if something goes wrong. For the next week they'll be turned upside down, round and round, and back to front.

They start in Gosport, at the Royal Navy's decompression chamber, learning about the effects of oxygen starvation at high altitude. The setting is pure World War Two. From the outside, the chamber looks like a bastardized piece of U-Boat technology – all pumps and valves. The Chief Petty Officer supervising the pressure settings calls out the altitude: '15 000 feet and rising.' Inside, the trainees are sitting on wooden-slatted benches on either side of the chamber, wearing old-fashioned oxygen masks. The sound of their slow, heavy breathing cuts through the clanking of the pumps, as air continues to be sucked from the chamber: '20 000 feet and rising.'

The decompression chamber is the last relic of Seafield Park, a training base which has been all but decimated by recent defence cuts. The Navy has closed the rest of the base down, but keeps the chamber operational because it makes money hiring it out to other branches of the military, such as the Army Air Corps. This is the new reality of post-Cold War life. Those buzzwords – 'cost-effectiveness', 'productivity', 'competitive tendering' – have reached deep into the heart of even the Armed Forces. The net result is eerie. There is no one else on the base, but the barbed wire and all the security paraphernalia are still intact, guarding nothing but an old decompression chamber clanking away.

'25 000 feet. Climb is complete.' The Chief Petty Officer and his safety team have done their job. Now the Army Air Corps' aero-medical expert, Lieutenant Colonel Malcolm Braithwaite, takes over. He asks the first pair, Corporal Jim LeCornu and Jenny Firth, to remove themselves from their oxygen supply and start doing simple tasks – drawing pictures, playing games, adding and subtracting. For the first few seconds they are fine, but within a minute they are losing control of their actions and becoming incapable of concentrating on any task (this is the effect of their motor-neurone systems slowing down through lack of oxygen). Jim is asked to draw an elephant, but it ends up as a wild and wonderful sea monster from the pages of Jules Verne. Jenny tries to do her sums, but after a while can't even subtract five from ten. They end up playing pat-a-cake, but find it hard enough to pat their own hands, let alone the hands of their partner. Meanwhile the rest of the trainees sit and watch, laughing as the two of them struggle to co-ordinate their movements.

Jenny is used to having the lads laughing at her; women don't survive long in the Army without knowing how to take a joke. 'I'm used to being the only woman in any organization I'm working in, and I've learned to expect a bit of teasing. You just have to give as good as you get.' There are plenty of people in the Corps who think it is a mistake letting women fly helicopters. They doubt whether women can cope with the pressure of the battlefield. They doubt whether women have the mental toughness it takes to command an aviation patrol. They doubt all sorts of things. But for the men on Course 354 the experience of working alongside Jenny for the first two and half months has been eye-opening. In a quiet way she has been very impressive as a trainee pilot and a course member, and she has quickly earned their respect. None of them was used to working with women, and they were apprehensive about having a female presence in the crewroom. But, besides moderating their language slightly, they have had to do little to accommodate her. Certainly, by now, none of them would dare suggest that Jenny wasn't worth her place on the course.

In the decompression chamber, the trainees are finding out how dangerous oxygen starvation is. Corporal Nigel Harrison and Lieutenant JP Miller are the next pair to come off oxygen. Like Jim and Jenny, they are asked to do some writing and simple mental arithmetic. They are told to remember a three-

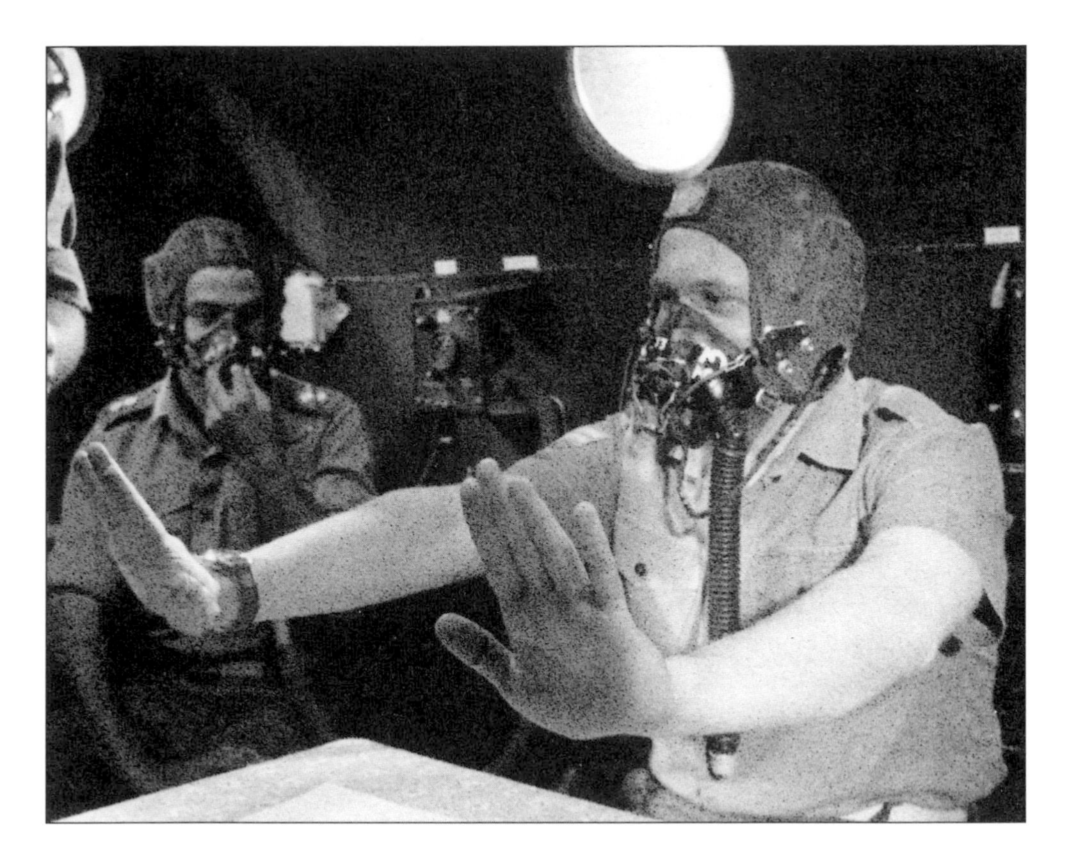

Oxygen starvation slows the flow of blood to the extremities. After a couple of minutes at 25 000 feet the trainees' fingers start turning blue.

digit number. After two minutes, Malcolm Braithwaite gives each of them a pile of plastic shapes and a ball with different shaped holes cut into its lid. It's a toy familiar to any toddler. 'All you have to do is put the right shapes in the right holes. Child's play.'

JP Miller goes straight for the container and starts dropping the plastic pieces into the right holes. But Nigel Harrison just sits there, staring blankly out in front of him. The Colonel repeats the command, but there's still no reaction from Nigel. He's displaying classic symptoms of hypoxia (the medical name for oxygen starvation). He is still fully conscious, but his brain has shut down, unable to process the information it's being given.

As soon as the Colonel realizes what has happened, he orders Corporal Harrison to plug himself back into the oxygen supply. Again, Nigel doesn't respond. He just holds the same blank stare. Another trainee helps him out and reattaches the umbilical tube that links his face mask to the main oxygen system. Initially, nothing happens and Nigel continues in his dream state, but gradually colour starts returning to his face and he comes to, unsure of what has happened. He sits rather sheepishly watching Lieutenant JP Miller – still off oxygen, but unaffected by hypoxia – carrying out the rest of the tasks set by the Colonel.

Half an hour later, the exercise is over and the trainees have returned to normal atmospheric pressure. Only now does Nigel start to smile again:

> I remember everything up to the second game of noughts and crosses, but nothing after that. When he asked us to write down the number he had given us at the beginning of the exercise, I thought he was bluffing because I couldn't remember any number.

The Colonel drives home the lesson to the rest of the group. What happened to Corporal Harrison after only two minutes without oxygen could have happened to any of them. In a decompression chamber such a reaction poses no great threat, but if any of them had been piloting an aircraft and suffered in the same way, the aircraft would probably have crashed and they would have died. Hypoxia seems amusing in a training exercise, but in real life it is lethal.

The course leave Seafield Park and head for the main training base in Gosport and more lectures about the physiological effects of flying. The Chief Petty Officer and his team stay behind and prepare the decompression chamber for the next day's run. They have the worst job. It takes great bravery to enter a decompression chamber after an exercise – the smell is unbelievable. One of the effects of pressure change on the human body is to expand the volume of internal gas. The gas has only one way of escaping, out of people's backsides. For an hour the ten trainees were farting continually, making a massive contribution to methane emissions in the Gosport area. It will take a good hour to clear the atmosphere in the decompression chamber.

Wednesday, 18 May

RNAS Yeovilton, Somerset

The next venue for survival week is RNAS Yeovilton, home of the Underwater Escape Unit, more commonly known as 'the Dunker'. It's a feared torture weapon, the modern equivalent of the dunking chair used to punish medieval witches. The trainees from Course 354 have heard all about it and they enter the building with some trepidation. There in front of them, suspended above a swimming pool is the fuselage of a helicopter connected to a crane. It can be raised and lowered at will and, because it is attached to a rotating cradle, it can also be spun upside down. At the moment it is sitting high above the pool, out of harm's way. On the wall there is a mysterious slogan painted in bold red letters. It demands 'Self-Determination Now!'

The course are here to learn the correct ditching procedure in the event of a helicopter crash at sea. Most fatalities in such crashes are caused not by the impact but by people drowning, unable to escape the aircraft. Therefore all military pilots have to visit the Dunker and practise different ways of escaping in simulated crash scenarios. No one is allowed to fly a helicopter over water unless they've done the training – and passed it.

After a briefing from the Chief Petty Officer, the trainees change from their fatigues into a thick rubber dry suit and crash helmet. They also strap on a personal survival pack which contains a small inflatable life raft. They're not going to use the life raft in the swimming pool, but they do the drill in the same kit that they would be wearing if they were flying a mission at sea.

Corporal Marcus Lock is dreading this exercise. He's a bad swimmer, and the thought of being stuck in a helicopter fuselage underwater, and spun upside down, fills him with horror. He changes into his dry suit and watches as the Dunker is lowered to water level and the first pair of trainees swim out to it. He has made sure that he'll be in the last pair to go, so that he'll know exactly what to expect when it comes round to his turn.

The first pair, Bombadier Stoneman and Corporal Hitch, are helped into the pilot and co-pilot seats of the Dunker by the two safety divers who give them their final instructions: 'That's your exit. Pull yourself out. Don't swim in the module or you'll kick each other. Only release the buckle when you're about to leave.' The divers then tell the Chief Petty Officer at the controls that they're ready for the first run.

He presses a button to raise the Dunker about 10 feet above water level, lets it sit there for a moment, and then presses another to bring it crashing down into the water, allowing it to drop 12 feet below the surface. Once the Dunker is at its lowest point, Corporals Stoneman and Hitch are allowed to unstrap their seat belts and escape.

The divers help them back into the module for their second run. This time it drops in the same way, but once it is underwater it spins over to simulate a helicopter capsizing. On the third run the poolside lights are turned off and the exercise is carried out in semi-darkness. On the fourth, and final, run every light in the building is turned off, and the trainees have to feel their way out in complete darkness. The biggest problem is just working out where the surface is. It is very easy to become disoriented when you're spinning upside down, unable to see anything at all.

Stoneman and Hitch manage all four runs without incident. As they swim to the poolside they look rather pleased with themselves; they even look as if they enjoyed it. The next pair dive into the water and swim over to the Dunker. Corporal Lock continues to watch closely. Having seen what's involved, he's relieved that it doesn't seem as difficult as he imagined. At the same time he's worried that if everyone else copes as easily as the first pair it will be even more embarrassing if he struggles. He's starting to regret being in the last pair to go, because it's given him more time to fret.

Sure enough, when Corporal Lock eventually does get his go, he has worked himself up into a state of anxiety. He has watched everyone else complete the drill. Now they'll all be watching him, waiting for something to go wrong. The Chief Petty Officer senses Marcus's anxiety and plays on it by taking the Dunker up higher than normal and holding it there longer.

High above the pool, Marcus looks down nervously, wondering when the drop will come. He applied for the course to escape the routine of life in the Light Infantry ('It's all digging trenches and shooting people') and saw flying as an exciting new challenge. But he didn't bargain for this. He sits there, thinking, 'Why did I ever agree to come on this course?.... Oh well, it's a good way of ending my career – "Corporal Lock drowned in swimming pool". Wonderful!'

With a jolt, the Dunker descends. Marcus takes a deep breath and suddenly he's underwater. He tries to remember what they told him to do, but struggles to unbuckle the strap. He practised the action over and over while he was waiting but now, when it matters, he can't get it open. In panic he starts tugging at it, but he's only making the strap tighter. Eventually a safety diver has to release him. He breaks the surface with a gasp of relief. But there's no respite. The other diver is waiting for him.

'Straight back into the module for the second run,' he says, and then asks as an afterthought, 'Are you OK?'

'No!' Marcus replies, trying his hardest to tread water and keep his head above the surface. The diver decides Marcus is joking and bundles him back into the module.

On the second run, Marcus sits with his hand on the strap buckle. He is determined to make a quick exit this time. But he's too quick. Once the Dunker drops to its lowest point, he unbuckles himself straight away, forgetting that on this run the module turns over. As it starts to spin, he falls out of his seat and is tossed around for a few seconds. He ends up on his side, uncertain where the exit is. His partner Nigel Harrison helps by giving him a push in the right direction. But, as Marcus tries to escape, the survival pack on his back gets caught in the door frame. It takes another shove from Nigel to free him. He's only been underwater for twelve seconds, but because the adrenaline is pumping, he breaks the surface gasping.

By the third run, Marcus is getting used to the Dunker. He's learnt how to time his exits properly. Surprisingly, he finds the final run – in pitch darkness – the easiest. 'As it was going down, I didn't have time to do my clasp up, so I just held on to the straps, waited for them to rock it, and then shot straight out the door.' When the lights come back on, he looks a considerably happier man. He's done it and, although it wasn't exactly pleasurable, he's survived all four runs. He takes some comfort from the knowledge that once he becomes a pilot he won't have to repeat Dunker training for at least two years. And when he does it again, at least he'll know what to expect.

Friday, 20 May

RAF St Mawgan, Cornwall

Course 354 have continued their travels westward, all the way to RAF St Mawgan, near Newquay in Cornwall. They're here to do the second half of their sea survival drill. In the Dunker they learnt how to escape from a helicopter in the event of a crash; here they're learning how to stay alive long enough to be rescued. They arrived at St Mawgan yesterday and spent the afternoon practising the drill in the relative comfort of the gymnasium. Today they've got to do it for real, in the sea.

If the course had reckoned that a date in late May would mean calm weather and an easy ride, then they were mistaken. It's a filthy day – the last remains of winter rather than the first hint of summer. It's cold and windy; so windy it was touch and go whether they'd set sail at all. But a final decision has been made and now Course 354 are on an RAF launch chugging into the English Channel, uncertain of what lies ahead. They

Any potential pilot must know how to survive a helicopter crash at sea. Course 354 practise the drill in the English Channel. First they jump in …

cheer themselves with a spontaneous, if half-hearted, rendition of 'Jerusalem'. Slowly they chug on.

After forty minutes, Squadron Leader Gordon Blackburn, the RAF Safety Officer, decides they are in a suitable spot, away from other ships and away from the shelter of the land. The waves are swelling to 10 feet, and the lunacy of what's about to happen suddenly hits the trainees. They are going to jump – voluntarily – into these waves, on the sort of day when no sane person should be at sea. They will then have to stay in the water on their own for as long as it takes an RAF helicopter to come and rescue them. Their only two aids in this venture are a life jacket and survival pack. When inflated, the survival pack transforms into a single person life raft, which they should get into as quickly as possible. They have been told to try and make themselves secure in their life rafts within three or four minutes, because hypothermia can start setting in after that. On dry land yesterday three or four minutes was ample time; here at sea it seems absurdly optimistic.

Squadron Leader Blackburn summons up the first two people to take the plunge.

... then they scramble into personal life rafts.

Marcus Lock has volunteered to go first this time, having learnt from his mistake at the Dunker. He is jumping in with Andy James. The Squadron Leader stands them on the edge of the launch and explains the procedure: 'When I say jump, you jump. And if you don't, you get a push.' He laughs with mock malice and orders the skipper of the boat to increase speed to simulate the impact of a real crash. Once they're at full power, he turns to Andy and Marcus, pats them on the back and gives them the fateful order: 'Jump!' Marcus jumps rather limply into the wake of the boat, Andy makes a decent stab at a somersault. Within seconds both are lost in the waves.

To Marcus's intense relief, his lifejacket inflates on cue. He has the comfort of knowing that, whatever else happens, at least he won't drown. Remembering what he's been taught, he pulls the catch on his survival pack and watches the pressurized gas canister do its work. Within a couple of seconds a bright red life raft appears in front of him. But to call it a life raft is misleading; it has the size and appearance of a heavy-duty sleeping bag. And, like a sleeping bag, it takes some getting in to. At the moment it's upside down, trying hard to cut itself adrift from Marcus and make a dash for the Atlantic Ocean. But Marcus somehow manages to turn it over and manoeuvre himself alongside, so that with one heave he can roll himself on to it. It's taken him three minutes just to get to this point. It takes another three to clamber into the life raft. Thankfully, the water isn't cold enough today to induce hypothermia.

While Marcus has been struggling to sort out his life raft, the rest of the course have followed him into the sea, two at a time. They all have the same problems negotiating the wind and the swell, but gradually they manage to clamber into their life rafts and make themselves relatively secure. Their next task is to avoid sinking. They're manically bailing out water, trying not to topple over in the process. Some of them drift close to each other and manage to share a few words of encouragement, before they drift apart again.

On the launch they are having their own problems. They've heard on the radio that the rescue helicopter has had a technical problem and can't come out to meet them. They're not entirely convinced. They suspect the pilot has taken one look at the weather and decided he's better off on the ground. Whatever the reason, the exercise isn't going to have its grand finale, and the trainees aren't going to have the dubious pleasure of being winched into a helicopter. They'll be picked up by the safety boat instead.

By now, the ten life rafts are happily bobbing up and down, stretched in a long, irregular line across the horizon. The trainees have done all the work. They've made themselves secure and relatively dry; now they just have to sit and wait. This is harder than it sounds. With nothing to do, there are no distractions. Suddenly they have nothing to think about except the one awful thought: I am going up and down, up and down, up and down. Am I going to be seasick? And the more they think about being sick, the more likely it is that they will be sick. As it happens, the only one to succumb is Corporal Mickey Rooney. He was teased on the journey out for eating too much; the others told him he was 'the fat boy from hell' and he was going to suffer and, sure enough, he did – all over his life-jacket and life raft.

After half an hour, Squadron Leader Blackburn sends out the safety boat to collect them and their rafts. They return to the launch elated. Even Marcus Lock has a smile on his face. For all the wilful disobedience of his life raft, he found this exercise a lot more fun than the Dunker. At least it was spent on the surface of the water and not underneath. The only person who doesn't look happy is Mickey Rooney. He's a disconsolate figure, sitting on the deck with lumps of sick stubbornly adorning his lifejacket. His gaze is fixed on the horizon and his mind is fixed on returning to dry land. All he is willing to say about the day's proceedings is: 'If I'd wanted to go to sea I would have joined the Navy, I didn't become an Army pilot for this.... Thank God it's over.'

Unfortunately it's not over yet. In picking up the life rafts, the safety boat has managed to get its propeller wrapped around one of the lines. It is unable to return under its own steam and has to be towed slowly back by the launch. A journey which previously took forty minutes, takes two hours this time. Two hours of buffeting by wind and swell is enough to upset the best of moods and, by the time the two boats finally limp into port, Course 354 are glad to say goodbye to the RAF, the Cornish coast and the English Channel. They've had enough of survival training. It's been an interesting week, but now they're ready for the main event. From Monday they'll be flying helicopters.

Monday, 23 May

Middle Wallop, Hampshire

A light shower passes over Middle Wallop, but the sun is still shining. A rainbow has appeared and, whether by accident or design, it forms a perfect arch over the main dispersal area. Beneath it, ten helicopters are on the tarmac, waiting for their pilots.

'This is the day you've been looking forward to. You want to become helicopter pilots and today you'll get your hands on the controls of a helicopter for the first time.' The ten trainees are in a briefing room, being addressed by Bob Weston. 'You'll always remember this phase of your training. One does. It's a very intense, very clear stage of your flying career.'

Bob Weston is the Chief Pilot on Basic Rotary training. Like Fred Trowern, his counterpart on Fixed Wing, he heads a team of civilians employed by an outside company, Bristows, to supply training and technical support. But there the comparisons end. Whereas Fred is a flamboyant figure, with an obvious love for flying that is apparently undimmed by age, Bob is a more workaday character. He does the job efficiently but is unable to communicate the same passion. When Fred met the course for the first time, he enthused them with stories of derring-do in the air, and promised them that: 'Flying is the best fun you can have with your clothes on'. By contrast, Bob's opening brief is full of meticulous detail; it's all timings, numbers and dates. The trainees dutifully write everything down, but they're impatient to get airborne.

They don't have to wait much longer. Once the brief is over, they meet up with their new instructors and head straight out to the tarmac. Jenny Firth has been assigned to Peter Earnshaw, who is the Deputy Chief Pilot. He is a slight man – shorter than Jenny – who seems very serious. He's certainly not a man for smalltalk, and their conversation is the stuff of technical manuals.

'The Gazelle was designed by the French in the 1970s.... It's powered by a turbine fuel-driven engine generating 592 shaft horsepower.... It's 31 feet long and weighs 2000 kg.' Jenny is getting her first formal introduction to the Gazelle, the helicopter she will be learning to fly for the next nine months. 'It has a top speed of 168 knots, but we tend to cruise at 120.... You'll notice it has a distinctive enclosed tail rotor, which is called a fenestron.'

The Army Air Corps bought the Gazelle in 1974 because of its reputation as a light, manoeuvrable helicopter, ideal for battlefield reconnaissance. It carries no weapons; its function is to seek out the enemy, observe him without being observed, and call down fire from other aircraft or ground-based guns. The trainees will be learning these skills later on in the course. They'll spend the next four months on Basic Rotary, just learning to fly it.

Mr Earnshaw has shown Jenny how to strap into the right hand seat of the helicopter, the pilot's seat. He is alongside her in the left-hand – co-pilot's – seat, taking her through the take-off drill. At this stage it means nothing to her – lots of buttons and mumbo-jumbo – nor is it meant to. The first flight is just for fun. It is the only unassessed sortie on the whole course, a chance to fly in the pilot's seat of a Gazelle for the first time and find out what it can do.

Mr Earnshaw takes off and they are away. Soaring high, then diving low. Skimming trees and hugging contours. They approach Harewood Forest, spot a tiny clearing and drop into it, clearing the trees by inches rather than feet. Suddenly they're up high again, and they stop. Dead still into a hover. They do a complete pirouette, have a look at the view and carry on. A steep bank, a pedal turn, a wingover. Jenny is enthralled: 'The freedom, the exhilaration, that feeling of being in complete control, being able to stop, go up, go down, turn around, being so versatile... it's wonderful!'

Then it's her turn. They're cruising at 1000 feet, away from any other traffic, and Mr Earnshaw invites Jenny to take control of the collective, a lever located on the cockpit floor to the left of the pilot, in the same position as a handbrake in a car. Jenny tentatively brings her left hand down from her lap on to the lever.

'Get a good grip about halfway down and just try to hold us level at this height. Nothing fancy.' Mr Earnshaw looks over to check that Jenny has her hand in the right place and lets go of his duplicate collective.

'You have control.'

'I have control, Sir.'

Jenny is flying the helicopter for the first time. Or, more accurately, she is controlling its height. There are three main controls on a helicopter – the collective, the cyclic and the pedals – and Mr Earnshaw is introducing them one at a time. 'Just keep it steady.... Do you see we're descending, so raise the collective a bit and we'll climb.... That's it.' Jenny is looking intently at the horizon, trying to fix it steady in her field of vision, conscious of every movement she makes with her left hand. Suddenly the lessons they've had about the aerodynamics of a helicopter start making sense.

Above her, spinning at 380 rpm, are three rotor blades, forming a disc. The only way a pilot can control the disc is by changing the pitch – the angle – at which the blades spin. The collective lever changes the angle of all the blades together (collectively) – hence its name. Lift it up and the blades increase their angle and the helicopter climbs. Lower it and the angle decreases and the helicopter descends.

Before the end of the flight, Jenny has a go on the other controls. First the cyclic. This is a control stick rising vertically from the cockpit floor between the pilot's legs. Move it left or right and the nose of the helicopter heads left or right. Move it forward or back and the nose drops or rises. Like the collective, it affects the pitch of the disc, but it does so cyclically rather than collectively. The blades increase their pitch in one half of their cycle, while feathering in the other half. This cyclic change of pitch causes the disc to tilt forward, backward, left or right and change the attitude of the helicopter.

Finally, the pedals. A side-effect of the clockwise motion of the blades, is a counter-force wanting to pull the helicopter fuselage anti-clockwise. This force is known as torque and needs to be compensated for by an anti-torque rotor (the tail rotor enclosed at the end of the fuselage). When it is spinning it pushes the tail sideways against the torque, and keeps the helicopter flying in a straight line. The yaw (the amount of push of the helicopter) is controlled by the pedals. Pressing the left pedal reduces the pitch angle of the tail rotor blades. This

The months of waiting are over. Jenny Firth is piloting a helicopter for the first time.

pushes the tail to the right against the torque and the nose of the helicopter yaws to the left. The right pedal increases tail rotor pitch and allows the torque to pull the aircraft right.

Jenny has learnt all this in the classroom, but it is so different doing it for real. Each control seems so much more sensitive than she imagined and so much more difficult to handle. She realizes that any advantage she had at the Fixed Wing stage is now firmly wiped out. She's starting from scratch, along with the others: 'I'm right down at the bottom, feeling jealous of those who have had any experience of a helicopter. It's going to be hard work, but hopefully it'll be fun while we're learning.'

After the flight Jenny returns to the crewroom, meets up with the rest of the course, and compares notes. Their reactions are much the same: a mixture of awe and excitement. Marcus Lock is particularly enthusiastic: 'It is totally different from anything I've done in my life. It's brilliant. You're up there with no idea of what anything does and you have control of this machine.

And your instructor is going "aagh!". It's absolutely brilliant.'

The only sour note for Marcus is a summons to see the Regimental Sergeant Major. He has been reported for an incident at St Mawgan last week. The evening he arrived at the base, he wanted to buy a soft drink from a vending machine, put his money in, but nothing came out. So he gave the machine a kick in frustration. One of the clerical staff spotted him and told him off, whereupon Marcus – allegedly – told her to get lost. It seemed a minor incident at the time, but it has now got all the way to the RSM, who tells him in no uncertain terms that he has demonstrated poor judgment and a lack of self-discipline – two qualities he will need in abundance if he is to become an army pilot.

An investigation will follow and, pending its results, Marcus will face a fine and possibly even dismissal from the course. He awaits his fate.

Wednesday, 25 May

The first few sorties on Basic Rotary are designed to consolidate the operation of the three controls. The trainees have to keep practising until the actions become instinctive: the left hand always moving up and down; the right hand making small circles over the knee; the feet pumping back and forth. But, more importantly, the actions have to become simultaneous, so that all three controls move together, not separately. If one control is moved, the other two have to be altered to compensate.

Every manoeuvre, even the simplest, must be thought of in three dimensions. For instance, to make a helicopter climb, one needs to increase the pitch angle of the disc with the collective lever, and pull more power. But more power creates more torque, so add more right pedal. More right pedal will yaw the aircraft right, so move the cyclic left. Only then will the helicopter climb properly. The same is true, in reverse, for a descent. Lower the lever, less power, more left pedal, more right cyclic.

It doesn't matter at this stage whether the trainees understand the aerodynamics, just as long as they understand that the controls are connected and their hands and feet need to move in sync. They're like actors learning a new part, taking advantage of every spare moment – in the hangars, crewrooms or messes – to go over the routines again and again. For these first days they are living, eating and breathing helicopters.

Bob Weston, the Chief Pilot, looks on. He's been at Middle Wallop long enough to recognize the pattern.

> At the moment they're excited. They're flying helicopters at last. But in our experience this high is usually followed by a dip when they realize how much they have to learn and how little time they'll have to learn it. We'll soon start seeing some furrowed brows as the trainees have to reproduce what their instructors are showing them.

Chapter Three

Solo

Monday, 6 June

Middle Wallop, Hampshire

In a corner of the airfield four helicopters are dancing an improbable dance. One moves right, the other goes left; one climbs to 20 feet, another drops to 6 inches. This is Course 354 learning to hover.

Each of the trainees has been allocated a 20-metre square marked out on the grass with creosote. Their task for today and the rest of the week is simple: just keep the aircraft within the confines of the square. The instructors call them 'torture squares' and the trainees are starting to find out why. A helicopter is inherently unstable. It wants to do anything but stay still. The only way to stop it wandering is by using all three controls to fight against each other. Move one and the other two have to be moved to compensate. It's a test of co-ordination and concentration.

'See the tree straight ahead? I want you to keep pointing at it? I'll have the cyclic and lever, you just have the pedals. OK?'

'Yes, Sir.'

'You have control.'

'I have control, Sir.' No sooner are the words uttered than they are rendered meaningless. Staff Sergeant Mark Finch clearly doesn't have control. Five seconds ago the Gazelle was static, floating happily 10 feet above the ground. Now it is swinging wildly from side to side. And the tree is moving in and out of Mark Finch's field of view.

'Sorry, Sir, it's going everywhere.'

'Don't worry, just feel your way through it. Nice and gentle.' Dave Stewart, the instructor, is far too experienced to get flustered. 'Smaller movements, just minor adjustments, very gentle.' Mr Stewart has perfected the instructor's art of looking completely calm even when a helicopter is seesawing aimlessly across the sky. He's shadowing Mark's every movement – just in case – but resisting the temptation to take over.

Slowly the pendulum movement of the Gazelle calms down and Mark succeeds in keeping the tree more or less in front of him. 'That's good. OK, I have control.' Mr Stewart takes the pedals from Mark. 'Right, now I'll have the pedals and cyclic. I want you to have a go with the lever. Just try and keep us at this height.'

Mark takes the lever and again struggles to control the aircraft. The tree immediately starts yoyo-ing up and down. But with gentle coaxing Mark starts to appreciate the sensitivity required and returns the aircraft to the level. Similarly when he takes the cyclic he lunges forward and backwards for a while until he gets a feel for it, but then manages to keep a relatively steady distance from the tree. Rather than simply chasing each movement, it is a matter of anticipating what the helicopter wants to do and correcting before it does it.

'Lovely. Now the real test. You're going to see what it's like with all three controls together. Remember, you've got to think of them working as one. OK?'

'Yes, Sir. I have control.' Cyclic in right hand, lever in left and pedals glued to his feet, Mark is holding his first hover. One... two... three... For three seconds he controls the helicopter fine, then a nudge of the cyclic and he starts scooting forward. He tugs back on the cyclic, but the aircraft starts climbing. He tries to compensate by lowering the lever but it yaws to the right, so he applies a bit of left pedal and it spins around to the left. Now he's too low so he lifts the lever and climbs again.

Ten seconds into the hover and Mark Finch is 30 feet above the ground, pointing at right angles to the tree, about 100 yards from the square. And the further from the target he drifts, the tighter he grips the controls and the less likely they are to have the desired effect. Afterwards he compares hovering in a helicopter with balancing an egg on its end on a mirror.

After thirty seconds, Mr Stewart takes control of the Gazelle.

Mark Finch has spent half his life in the Army. He's looking for a new challenge.

The beast is suddenly tamed, and returns obediently to the starting square. 'That wasn't too bad for a first go,' says Mr Stewart. Mark looks relieved, but a little disbelieving. 'We tell you to keep it within the square, but we're happy at this stage if you just keep it in the county. The only thing is, you must try and relax a bit more.' This is not the first time – and certainly won't be the last – that Mark Finch has been told to relax.

In the crewroom after the flight, Mark fills in his logbook. To look at, he's the typical soldier: crewcut hair, thickset features, a flattened nose that's probably been broken a couple of times. He also sounds like a soldier: clipped short sentences, tending to the monosyllabic. When you ask him about his motives for coming on the course he gives the stock answers: 'I want to fly because it's a logical extension of my military skills.... The helicopter is the teeth-arm weapon of the future...'

But there's something that doesn't quite fit about this soldier. No matter how professional and detached he tries to sound, his eyes tell a different story. They're too sad and too vulnerable to be soldier's eyes. They're the eyes of a man desperately seeking something new. It seems odd to talk of a thirty-two-year-old having a mid-life crisis, but that's what Mark Finch is facing.

He joined the Army when he was sixteen and signed up for the full twenty-two years. Like any young soldier, he joined for the travel, adventure and camaraderie. He started as a private and worked his way up the ranks, serving in Northern Ireland, Cyprus and Germany. He became a staff sergeant in the Royal Signals – his reward for keeping his nose clean, working hard and doing exactly what was expected of him. His career has been a story of steady progress, nothing spectacular but always solid. In Army terms he is 'a safe pair of hands'.

But Mark has now spent half his life in the Army and the appeal has started to wear thin. He finds it hard to put his finger on what's missing, all he knows is that he doesn't get the same buzz any more. He's lost that feeling of being part of a team, with everyone pulling together. He also fears he's progressed about as far up the ranks as he's ever likely to go in the Signals. He needs a change, a new challenge – hence his desire to become a pilot.

He tried to get on the pilot's course three years previously, but didn't make it through selection. He then married and put aside any ambitions to fly. He concentrated instead on trying to make his marriage work. But his wife didn't like the itinerant nature of Army life, and they separated within a year, leaving Mark alone, another soldier who couldn't make his military and domestic lives work in sync.

In 1993 he tried the Corps again. He knew he was right at the top of the age limit for pilot training, so this would be his last chance. To his delight and some surprise he was accepted on to Course 354. Here was an opportunity to put his failed marriage behind him and rediscover that missing spark in his career. Here was an opportunity to start anew.

> This is what I want to do in the Army now, and if I don't achieve it I've got a couple of stark choices to make. Either I get out or I go for a completely different trade within the Army. I don't want to go back to what I was doing.

Small wonder that Mark finds it hard to relax. He alone knows how much he's invested in the course.

Wednesday, 8 June

The rush is on. Middle Wallop is bathed in sunshine and the instructors want to take advantage of the weather to push the course through their basic training as quickly as possible. The first challenge is to get all the trainees solo within eleven hours of tuition. As with Basic Fixed Wing, it involves a lot of circuit-bashing: taking off, flying a rectangular circuit of the airfield at 700 feet, landing, taking off and doing another circuit, and another and another. The routine is only broken by practice forced landings. The Army Air Corps teaches its pilots to fly helicopters as if the engine might quit at any moment.

A forced landing is genuinely scary. The instructor cuts the engine and the helicopter is in freefall. The rotor blades naturally slow down to a stop and the helicopter drops like a stone unless the trainee manages to push the lever down immediately and flatten the pitch angle. With the pitch flat, the rotors continue spinning and provide some lift while the helicopter descends like a sycamore seed. This process is called auto-rotation. At 50 feet from the ground the trainee pulls back on the cyclic, causing the nose of the aircraft to flare. This flaring action is meant to slow the speed of the helicopter from 60 knots to zero. Just before the tail hits the ground, the trainee lifts the lever and pushes the cyclic forward a little to level off the aircraft and glide into a smooth landing.

That's the theory. In practice, trainees new to auto-rotation are thrown by 'ground rush'. Lieutenant Jenny Firth is typical. She starts descending at the right speed and carries out the proper drills but at the critical moment, about five seconds from touchdown, she looks down and sees the green of the airfield trying to envelop her cockpit. Her reaction is natural – she freezes. 'Ooh it's all coming up so quick...so quick.... Aah, I've forgotten it all.' Her instructor, Mr Earnshaw, takes control, and lands safely. Jenny is reminded again of the difference between the classroom and the cockpit. On the ground she has been through the drill over and over again; she knows exactly what to do. In the air, when she's falling at 2000 feet a minute, it all disappears. Jenny knows she won't be going solo until her forced landings have become instinctive.

Mark Finch is also having problems with auto-rotation. But

for him there's a bigger problem, a growing lack of confidence. He seems incapable of dictating terms to the helicopter; it's controlling him, rather than vice versa. His instructor, Mr Stewart, is trying to build his confidence by getting him to talk his way through everything he does. 'Keep saying to yourself, "Flare, flare, flare, check level, run on".' Mark mutters the mantra to himself over and over while he's cruising at height, but once the descent starts his focus goes. 'Flare... flare... eh... come on... whoa.' Mark hasn't managed to slow the aircraft enough and the skids thump the ground before sliding a further 20 yards on the grass.

'Sorry, Sir, but at least we're down.'

Mr Stewart chuckles. 'Yes, at least we're down.'

During the debrief Mark feels the need to offer some explanation for his poor flying. He reveals for the first time the personal problems he's having away from the course. It's a calculated risk: by being open about his private life he may give the system cause to question his professionalism, but if he stays quiet no one will understand the stress he's under. Having made the decision to talk, he reveals all.

Last week, he had a motorbike accident. His brand new Triumph 650 was bumped by one of the cars on the base. Now the insurance companies are refusing to pay the £300 repair bill. Mark fears he'll have to fork out himself or lose his no-claims bonus; either way, it'll cost money. More seriously, he's running into financial difficulty buying a flat. Wanting something tangible to show for his sixteen years in the Army, Mark decided to enter the property market and buy a one-bedroom flat in Andover, 5 miles from Middle Wallop. He had no problem finding the place or getting the mortgage, but he has been surprised by the solicitor's fees and all the extra up-front demands that have mounted up. Today he received a letter demanding another £450 immediately, or else he may have to forego the purchase. With nothing left in the bank, he has spent the non-flying part of the day trying to find the money, and has come up with two options – either cash in his life insurance policy at a considerable loss to him, or borrow the sum from his ex-wife. At the moment he favours the former option: it may be more drastic but at least it doesn't involve the embarrassment of asking his ex-wife.

The rush is on. Just eleven hours to go solo.

Mark now regrets ever having decided to buy the flat at a time when he should have been concentrating on the course and only the course. He knows the stress he's been feeling has affected his flying.

> Anything that disturbs your train of thought or distracts you from what you're meant to be doing on the course is a problem and should be avoided at all costs. Looking back it was probably a mistake to start buying a place now. I should have waited till after the course. I've learned my lesson – you need to be concentrating 100 per cent on flying all the time and I'll bear this in mind through the rest of the course.

Mark leaves the hangar after the debrief feeling a great sense of relief at having shared his problems. But he can't help wondering if he's made a mistake. What are they going to think of a potential battlefield pilot who gets stressed out by a few financial worries?

Back in his room in the sergeants' mess, he spends the evening flying – in his head. He turns his easychair into a cockpit seat and surrounds himself with imaginary controls. He then flies one imaginary circuit after another, talking himself through every manoeuvre, concentrating on every safety check, always consulting a set of imaginary dials for reference. And all the while he tries to forget about the £450, the flat, the estate agents, the solicitors, the ex-wife – everything except flying. 'I know I can fly, I know I can do it, but my instructor has hinted that we're running out of time. I just have to get my act together, take the bit between my teeth and do it.'

Wednesday, 15 June

The eleventh hour approaches. One by one the trainees are going solo: first Corporal Rooney, then Corporal Lock.

Lieutenant JP Miller, the ambitious Zimbabwean officer, should have been the next to make it, but he is foiled by a freak accident. Just as his instructor utters the immortal words 'one more good landing and I'll be getting out', his cockpit fills with smoke. The hot weather has caused the battery to overheat and catch fire. They put down, shut off the engine and walk away to safety. Seconds later, a fire engine and ambulance are racing across the airfield to the grounded helicopter. One team of men douses the fire, another team extricates the battery. They all take it very seriously, but for an emergency service that has experienced some horrific crashes at Middle Wallop, this is a pretty tame emergency. For JP, however, it's a first-hand reminder of how dangerous flying helicopters can be. They spend so much time preparing for the unexpected – now it's happened.

JP returns to the crewroom from his aborted flight and walks into a reception committee led by Andy James.

'Got a light?' asks Andy in feigned innocence. 'I smell smoke.'

'Very funny, very funny. Look what happens when you give anything to a Zimbabwean – they break it,' JP replies self-mockingly.

'We were watching you from here and I could see you land and I said, "Ah, JP's going solo". Then we waited and waited and saw the fire engine come out and thought, shit, what's going on?'

'I *was* about to go solo, then whoosh – flames everywhere. It was an act of God or something.'

At the same time, in another part of the airfield, Jenny Firth has touched down. Mr Earnshaw gives her some feedback on how she's been flying and then breaks the big news.

'Your circuit is still a bit ragged but that'll come with more practice. Your take-offs and landings are good and you've sorted out your engine-offs, so I'm going to pop out now and let you go on your own.'

'Oh no...' Jenny seems genuinely surprised, as if she has been so busy concentrating on the minutiae of flying her circuits, she's forgotten the bigger picture, the requirement to go solo within eleven hours. Mr Earnshaw unbuckles, opens his door and gets out of the helicopter.

'Just keep doing what you've been doing and you'll be fine. Happy?'

'Er, yes, Sir. Is there a look of fear on my face?' But Mr Earnshaw doesn't answer: either he doesn't hear the question or he chooses not to tell her. He closes the door and Jenny is on her own, in charge of a helicopter for the first time in her life.

Mr Earnshaw stands in front of the helicopter in Jenny's

ten o'clock field of view and, palms up, gestures for her to lift. She tries her hardest to pretend nothing is different, ignore his absence and fly as normal. She talks her way through take-off just as she has done a hundred times and heads into a blue sky, leaving her instructor standing on the airfield, an ever-smaller figure.

> You keep wanting to go solo, and you have to do yet another sortie and then another sortie. But when your instructor finally waves you off, you get a few butterflies in the stomach. At least you know he has faith that you can take yourself around a circuit and get back safely. I'm not sure I had that faith in myself.... But once you manage to do it, it's a big boost to your confidence for the other exercises you're going to have to do afterwards.

Thursday, 16 June

Today the rest of the trainees on Course 354 break the solo barrier. JP Miller manages it, without further incident. Andy James goes solo. Even Mark Hitch, who struggled so

Jenny is delighted. She has made it solo and can look forward to the next challenge.

badly on Fixed Wing, goes through with no problems this time.

By the end of the afternoon, the crewroom is buzzing with conversation about the joys of solo flying. Everyone has now flown their eleventh hour and they've all gone solo – all except Mark Finch. He is standing quietly in one corner of the room, watching the kettle boil, waiting for the fateful call. Sure enough, the phone rings. 'Staff Finch, this is Mr Weston. Can you come up to my office as soon as possible?' Mark gives up on the tea and makes his way upstairs.

Bob Weston makes a gentle headmaster. He starts by breaking the bad news. 'Following your flight today, I have had a word with your instructor and we have decided to place you on review.' But he spends the next ten minutes trying to cheer Mark up. 'We're all rooting for you.... You're a good chap, trying very hard, but you're not quite there.... We've got three extra hours to help you out.' Mark sits impassively, taking the news like a soldier. But again his eyes give him away. He knows that, whatever the formulation of words, he is on his way out unless he can improve his flying quickly.

Mark Hitch and Marcus Lock enjoy an evening drink having joined the solo club.

Mark leaves Bob's office, changes and gets straight on his bike. At this moment, he wants to be anywhere but Middle Wallop. He burns up the A343, heading for Andover and his flat. Here, at least, things have improved. His bank have allowed him to extend his overdraft by £450 and he's been able to complete on the purchase without either cashing in his life insurance policy or borrowing from his ex-wife. He picks up the keys from the estate agent and enters the flat for the first time as its owner. In different circumstances, this would be a proud and happy moment. As it is, he can't help wondering whether he'll be at Middle Wallop long enough to enjoy his new home.

He is welcomed by a bottle of wine and a note from the previous owners – 'DEAR MARK, GOOD LUCK IN YOUR NEW HOME'. He is touched by the gesture and sees it as evidence that things are starting to look up. With the flat sorted, he'll be able to concentrate full-time on flying. But they say trouble comes in threes... and, following the problems with his bike and then the flat, Mark has received more bad news. His stepfather died three days ago. Instead of starting tomorrow with the first of his review flights, he must go up to London and attend the funeral. He's been granted a day's compassionate leave.

> I will go to the funeral and mourn the loss of a nice guy. It's tragic, but it doesn't cause me any stress because it's not something I can do anything about, whereas the flat and trying to arrange the solicitor's fees was a problem of my own making, something that only I could sort out. Hopefully now the flat's sorted, my flying will follow suit.

Back at base, Mark spends another evening in his room practising his flying drills. For the first time he is aware of feeling alone – he's the only person on review. While the others will be moving on and learning new skills, he'll be repeating the same sorties until he goes solo. The sense of loneliness is made worse by being the only senior NCO on the course. The three officers can socialize with each other away from the course; the six corporals can do the same, sharing their trials and tribulations in the evening. But Mark Finch has no one else. There are sergeants from other courses in his mess, but they're all at different stages of their training. If he wants to meet up with any of the others on Course 354, the officers' mess is absolutely off limits. He can theoretically wander over to see the corporals in Hotspur House, but even this is frowned upon as over-fraternization with other ranks. It has been made clear to him that a senior NCO is not expected to mix with junior NCOs. So, instead, he sits in his room on his own, thinking about flying, hour after hour, unable to unload his worries.

Monday, 20 June

It's 11 a.m. and Mark Finch has just completed the first of his three review flights. He has a new instructor, Billy Campbell, but he is having the same old problems. He's too tense, too indecisive, and too easily distracted. Mr Campbell is shocked: 'His hands were wrapped around the controls very tightly. Some of his landings were dangerous. And he seems to be working at 100 per cent capacity.'

Mr Campbell wants Mark to do another flight as soon as possible. He's given him a couple of hours to prepare himself mentally, but he wants them to take off again by 1.30 p.m. Mr Campbell is from the 'if you fall off a horse get straight back up again' school of training. He doesn't want Mark to spend time dwelling on his problems and contemplating the worst.

Mark tries to relax in the crewroom with the others. It's a mistake. Corporal Hitch, whose confidence has grown enormously since his time on review, is playing with Hamish, the resident Hangar Three golden retriever. He's teasing him with a banana from his lunch box, offering it to him but then waving it out of reach. The others are joining in the fun. Mark just sits in his corner, unable to laugh with the rest of them. All he wants to do is study his safety checks before his flight.

At first glance the behaviour of the rest of the course seems indifferent, even callous. But that's wrong. They are all fond of Mark as a friend and respect him as an experienced senior NCO. It's just that they're completely absorbed in their own flying and their own problems. It's as if they've been thrown in at the deep end and told to swim. They're so busy just keeping their heads above water, they haven't got time to look out for the drowning man. Jenny Firth expresses the insecurity felt by the whole course:

> We don't want to see anyone on the course struggling; we want everyone to get through. So naturally we feel a bit guilty that we've been able to break the solo barrier whilst Staff Finch is struggling. But you have to realize that anybody can go on review for whatever reason and it's bound to be a shock – as I'll find out when it hapens to me. It's a system designed to help with your problems and get you back on course.

Mark takes off for his second flight, and there's an immediate improvement. He's more deliberate about what he's doing, more aware. Mr Campbell notices the change. 'The tension is gone and he's able to respond to me telling him what to do.' All the tuition, the encouragement, the hours of imaginary flying seem to be having some effect. Mark even looks a little less terrified in the cockpit.

He does a series of excellent take-offs and landings, his hovering has improved, his forced landings aren't perfect but at least they're safe. His biggest problem is general accuracy on the circuit work. If that had been better, Mr Campbell would have been tempted to send him solo. Certainly if he maintains the same rate of improvement he'll go solo tomorrow.

For the first time in days, Mark returns to his room with something resembling a smile on his face.

Tuesday, 21 June

Rain stops play. The spell of perfect weather breaks and gives way to a nasty squally front. Mark sits around the hangar waiting for the word to take off, but it never comes. By midday all flying is cancelled for the day. Mark's emotions are mixed. He's glad he wasn't required to fly in such bad weather – the forecast for tomorrow is much better. But he's annoyed to have lost the momentum. With the second of yesterday's flights fresh in his mind, he feels sure he could have repeated it, made the necessary improvements and gone solo. The agony would be over. Instead he must now wait another twenty-four hours and psych himself up again from scratch. 'The worst thing is the waiting. I just want to get out there and prove I can do it.'

Wednesday, 22 June

His fears are borne out. Today's third and last review flight follows the pattern of the first; he's too tense again. He flies like a man who has been up all night worrying. Whatever confidence he had, he has lost from one day to another. He blames the weather. If only he'd had been able to fly yesterday. If only....

Mr Campbell debriefs him and spells out the obvious. 'You were given three extra hours on review in which to go solo and you haven't been able to achieve that. I have no option but to hand you on to the military.'

As civilians, Mr Campbell and the other instructors on Basic Rotary are not in a position to decide on the fate of a trainee. They can suggest and recommend, but the final decision rests with the Army. Therefore, anyone who fails a review period is given one more flight with one of the senior military examiners. They call it a check ride – a final flight to confirm the assessment of the civilian instructor.

But there is still hope for Mark. If he flies well enough tomorrow, the military examiner will release him solo – check ride or not. He will then come off review and be allowed to continue training with the others. Admittedly this is not the likeliest of outcomes, but there are plenty of precedents. Middle Wallop is rich with stories of trainees unexpectedly passing their check rides and going on to complete the course, often ending up as top pilots. Mark can take some solace from these tales. He knows tomorrow is his last, last chance.

Thursday, 23 June

There is something beautiful about Middle Wallop in June. The green of the grass competing with the yellow of the buttercups. Blue sky with the occasional fluffy white cloud. And on dispersal, a dozen helicopters bask in the sunshine.

Mark Finch, however, is in no mood to admire the beauty around him. As he walks around his helicopter doing pre-flight checks, he can only think of one thing. This is his fifteenth flight in a helicopter, the fifteenth time he's checked the rotors, the engine, the filter, the transmission, the antennae, and all the rest. It may also be the last time.

Mark's check ride is being supervised by the Deputy Chief Flying Instructor, Squadron Leader Dave LeMare. He plays it very straight, like the typical driving test examiner: no small talk, no feedback, just clear precise instructions. 'I'd like you to start by hover-taxiing to the runway, taking off and flying an ordinary circuit before returning to the runway.' With a wobble Mark takes off and heads out to the runway in the middle of the airfield. He's telling himself: 'Relax, relax. It's easy. You know you can do it. Fly the first circuit well, then another, then another and he's bound to let you go solo. Just relax.' He soars into the blue sky, heading for one of the fluffy white clouds.

The first circuit is fine. He looks relieved as he returns to the runway. But, as he's preparing to head off on a second circuit, the DCFI throws him by asking him to demonstrate a landing. It's not an outrageous request – far from it – but he's so nervous that anything unexpected has the ability to throw him. Consequently, Mark makes a complete mess of it. The right skid hits the ground with a hefty bump, and the helicopter bounces up. Then the left skid hits and has the same effect on the aircraft. At the third attempt he manages to get both skids on to the ground and keep them there. Mark apologizes, 'I'm sorry, Sir, that was very bad. The worst one I've ever done. I wasn't expecting it.' The DCFI slips out of examiner mode and tries to reassure Mark. 'I'm sure you'd like to show me how you can do it properly. So fly another circuit and then have another go at landing when we get back here. OK?'

Surprisingly, the dreadful landing lifts some of the tension from Mark's flying. It is as if he realizes he's got nothing to lose. His second circuit is fine. He lands properly this time. On the third circuit he also does a reasonable emergency landing.

Outside the crewroom in Hangar Three an audience has formed. The rest of Course 354 have classes all morning, but this is their coffee break and they're taking the opportunity to watch the drama unfold out on the airfield. They watch as Mark comes in to complete his fourth circuit and cheer as he makes a good approach and landing. He takes off on a fifth circuit. They know that time is running out. The sortie has gone on for about forty minutes now. If Mark is going to have time to do a solo circuit, this

Before every flight the trainees carry out safety checks on the helicopter: rotors, engine transmission, filter. Nothing is left to chance.

needs to be his last dual circuit. One more good approach and landing and the DCFI will surely get out and let him go solo.

Up in the air, Mark has made the same calculation. He knows that his career is riding on this last circuit. Just five more minutes. He makes his first turn of the circuit and does his checks. Four minutes. He manages a downwind practice forced landing – in this drill the trainee finds a field to land in, makes the approach, but doesn't actually land. Three minutes. Mark returns to the circuit height and turns on to the base leg. Two minutes. The last turn on to finals and start the approach. One minute. Descend to the runway, holding the correct attitude and checking speed through descent.

Mark has completed another adequate circuit. His audience cheers. The DCFI is satisfied with Mark's circuit work, but wants to see him do one more landing before he sends him solo. Mark hears the instruction, but suddenly freezes. It's the pilot's equivalent of stage fright. All the anxiety, the stress and fear of the last week have crystallized into this moment. He just can't land. The audience are shouting, imploring him to touch down. He makes a crude attempt, but thinks better of it and drifts back to 6 feet. He tries again, but touches with only the right skid, before bouncing up again.

For a full minute he bounces up and down, trying to make the last landing. But all the time his hands are clutching the controls tighter and tighter and his movements become more and more clumsy. If a voice in his head could have just whispered, 'you've done this lots of times before, it's no big deal,' he moght have made the landing without problems. But the only voice he could hear was the one telling himself, 'come on... come on... you idiot... just do it... come on... now... come on...' In the end, Mark was defeated by nothing more complicated than pressure, pure self-induced pressure.

'I have control.' The DCFI takes over and puts Mark out of his misery. Mark takes his hands off the controls and strains to unclench his fingers, they've been wrapped so tightly around the cyclic and lever. The DCFI taxis the aircraft back to the dispersal. Mark says nothing. There's nothing to say.

'We saw your last landing. You were up, then down, then up. We were all rooting for you.' In the crewroom, Corporal Marcus Lock is trying to console Mark after the flight.

'Yeah, I was so close. If I'd just got that landing, I'm sure he would have got out and let me go solo.... Mind you he gave me a good crack at it, but I was just too nervous.'

'Don't worry. It's not over yet. They may decide to give you another hour.'

'Well, he said we've run out of time now. But they're going to look at my book and see how I've done across the whole course.'

'Don't worry. It's not over yet.'

Marcus Lock is wrong. It *is* over. While the trainees are talking in the crewroom, the DCFI is discussing the flight with the Chief Flying Instructor, Lieutenant Colonel David Patterson. It doesn't take the CFI long to come to a decision. Staff Sergeant Finch will never make an Army pilot. He has found too much of the course too hard, and the toughest part of the training is still ahead. The CFI consults the Commandant, Colonel Wawn, who is of the same opinion. Finch must go.

At 1.15 p.m. – an hour and a half after his last flight ended – Mark Finch marches into the CFI's office and salutes. 'Sit down Staff, take your beret off and relax.' This is positively the last time anyone at Middle Wallop is going to tell Mark to relax. He takes a seat and waits for the news. 'Right, we've come to the crunch. We've come up against the limit of your ability. You're operating at 100 per cent. There's no spare capacity there to learn new things.' Any glimmer of hope Mark had of a last-minute reprieve has disappeared. He knows full well where the CFI's line of argument is heading.

> We could probably get you solo if we gave you more hours, but this is only the first hurdle. There are plenty of bigger hurdles to come further down the course. If we were to let you carry on, the pressure you'd be under would just get worse and worse. It would be so great it would damage you. Therefore, taking everything into consideration, I have no option but to recommend you are suspended from flying training.

Mark is unable to believe what he's hearing. He's thought about little else than the possibility of being chopped, but now that it's actually happened he is still surprised. There's something so stark and final about that phrase, 'I have no option but to recommend you are suspended from flying training.'

Mark leaves the CFI's office and wanders back to the crewroom. Nine sets of eyes are fixed on him as he enters. He just shakes his head – he doesn't need to say anything. He sits down and starts packing up his flight bag. There is a moment of stunned silence, but then the others react as soldiers traditionally react to adversity. They take the piss. 'Oh well, one less place at the Wings Party.... Can I have your maps?... Back to the good old Royal Sigs, eh?' Mark takes the ribbing well. It seems odd to be laughing at this moment, but it's better than crying.

The black humour hides a real depth of feeling; the other members of Course 354 are genuinely upset. Once Mark has made a discreet exit from the crewroom, their true feelings come to the fore.

Bombardier Paul Stoneman is usually the quiet unflappable one, but today he's very vocal: 'It's a bitter blow. We're all very depressed. We feel like a piece of our anatomy has been hacked off. Morale is suddenly rock bottom as we realize there won't be ten people at the Wings Parade on 17 February.'

Andy James is just as upset: 'If he wasn't such a good bloke it wouldn't matter so much, but because he is a bloody good bloke and because he's the first to go it really does make you think, my God, that could be any of us.'

It's left to Jenny Firth to be more reflective about the first casualty of Course 354:

> It's very sad – he was a very important member of the course. But it's something we always knew might happen, and we've got to carry on. Morale is low right now, but we can't fall to pieces or we'll all go. I know Staff wouldn't want that.

Monday, 27 June

Mark is clearing his things out of the sergeants' mess. This is his last day at Middle Wallop and he's packing up his clothes and books. The tiny room which used to be crowded with his personal effects is now empty except for a solitary poster of the Army Air Corps display team, the Blue Eagles. There's an image of five display helicopters matted on to a golden sunset, and underneath it the caption reads 'IT'S A KIND OF MAGIC.' Mark has decided to leave the poster behind; the magic is tarnished.

He's feeling sad rather than bitter – sad because he'll have to give up flying. When he came on the course he claimed to be indifferent to the prospect of flying and talked about it as nothing more than a logical career move. Now, four months later, he's learned to love it. 'It's just being up there, being free, doing what you want to do. It's been terrific. Unfortunately that's all I can take away with me now, the experience of having flown.' He's asked about joining the Army's flying club where they fly light aircraft for fun – a poor substitute. He wanted to be a military helicopter pilot, not a Sunday afternoon enthusiast.

He's also sad because he'll miss life in the Army Air Corps. He came on the course feeling jaded and disillusioned with the Army. He was on the point of chucking it in. But four months at Middle Wallop have reinvigorated him: 'It's given me something I didn't bargain for – a kind of faith in the Army and human nature. It sounds silly, but I've gained that back again.' For a soldier who has spent sixteen years following orders and leaving the thinking to others, the atmosphere at Middle Wallop has been a revelation. 'Having come here and seen what life can be like – all the ranks working together, everybody keen to get on with the job, no hassle telling people what to do – it's been so heartening. It's changed me I suppose.' Here is the true tragedy. Mark came on Course 354 desperate for a new challenge and, to his delight, he found it in the skies around Middle Wallop. But just as he's settled into his new niche, he has to give it all up and return to the ways of old.

From tomorrow he'll resume his career with the Royal Signals, who will send him on a year's posting to Northern Ireland. When he started the course he vowed he wouldn't go back to the Signals. If he failed he'd either leave the Army or look for another role, anything but return to his old trade. Now that it's happened he's not so sure. He doesn't want to make any rash decisions, so in the short term he'll reluctantly accept his new posting. In the long term he says he'll think about his options. 'I'll take however long it takes to decide what I'm going to do next. Everybody's got to have a challenge. Sometimes you go a while till you find another one. But I'll find something else to go for.'

Fighting words, but realistically Mark's options are limited. If he leaves the Army he will find it hard to build a civilian

The Gazelle returns to the hangar; Mark Finch has flown his last flight.

career without qualifications. If he stays, he is thirty-two and considered old in Army terms, probably too old to receive any further training opportunities. Whatever spin Mark puts on his suspension, he knows in his heart that the pilot's course was his chance and he's blown it. Whatever he chooses to do now, it's going to be hard to bounce back.

Mark's bags are packed. He's returned his helmet and flying suit to the Quartermaster, and he's handed his books back to the Librarian. He wanders down the corridor of the sergeants' mess, says goodbye to the mess manager and walks out of the main entrance. As he leaves, he takes one last look over his shoulder, before shutting the door behind him. For Staff Sergeant Finch the dream is over.

Chapter Four

Flying Blind

Friday, 22 July

Middle Wallop, Hampshire

Summer is party season at Middle Wallop. The flying day usually finishes around five o'clock, so there are three or four hours of warm evening sunshine in which to throw a barbecue or drinks bash. Any excuse will do: the passing of an exam, a visit from family or friends, the end of the week. But tonight's party is special. It's the night of the Officers' Summer Ball, the social event of the year.

By six o'clock the mess is frantic. Officers are ironing their mess kit and polishing their spurs. Girlfriends are arriving, carefully cradling their ball gowns. The sculptor is putting the finishing touches to tonight's centrepiece – an Army Air Corps eagle carved out of ice. And the bar manager is checking his supply of champagne, ready for the bacchanalia to begin.

By eight o'clock all is calm efficiency. The officers are on the grass in front of the mess, drinking their first buck's fizz of the evening and making smalltalk while the sun sets. They are all dressed in their regimental mess kit: tight dark blue trousers and a dark blue jacket with light blue trim, black boots and spurs. The women are dressed more colourfully, in chiffon, silk and taffeta. At either end of the throng are two women who have unfortunately chosen exactly the same dress – a bold green and red tartan design – and they spend the rest of the evening trying to avoid each other.

The Army Air Corps band provides the evening with its one moment of gravitas by beating the retreat. At precisely

8.10 p.m., they line up in front of the flag pole and play 'Sunset', while the Corps flag is lowered. It's Army tradition, the ceremonial end of the day. The flag and the flag pole are treated with almost religious reverence. The Chief of Staff at Middle Wallop, Colonel McMahon, takes the salute, and the band march off, their duty performed. With impeccable timing, the mess manager appears and announces that dinner is served.

By ten o'clock a transformation has occurred. During dinner the revellers have managed to consume vast quantities of alcohol and they are now setting about the evening's entertainment in varying states of inebriation. The wise are treating it like a marathon, and are pacing themselves to survive all night. Others are sprinting from the off and already in danger of hitting the wall.

Jenny Firth comes into the latter category. She has taken to the dance floor with reckless abandon. There are three different sources of music: a DJ playing current chart hits, a four-piece band doing Abba covers, and a rockabilly combo trying to look cool amid the chaos. Jenny is not fussy, she is dancing to all of them. Everyone looks surprised at her behaviour, because she is normally so reserved, but tonight she's determined to let her hair down – at least metaphorically speaking. In fact, no matter how much she drinks, her hair stays scraped back into its ponytail for the duration of the evening.

Andy James is neither sprinting nor pacing himself. He's doing both. He's treating the evening as a series of short alcoholic sprints interspersed with bouts of quiet exhaustion. He's determined to be the last person still awake tomorrow morning. His guest is his new girlfriend, the raven-haired Vanessa. They are very much in love, and although he's only twenty-one, he's convinced this is the real thing. At this stage of the evening the two are inseparable, dancing together as close as they dare, mouthing the words of 'One Night in Heaven' to each other.

While the officers are dancing at the ball, Bombardier Paul Stoneman is on guard duty. He can just about hear the music from the guardroom, but it's a world from which he and the other men are excluded. The closest he gets to it is an hourly once-over of the perimeter fence, checking for any strange goings on. It's not clear whether he's trying to protect the officers from the outside world or vice versa. Whatever, it's a boring way to spend a Friday night, but one he accepts with his usual wryness: 'The officers go to the ball and Cinderella gets to stand guard.'

The rest of the corporals on 354 are enjoying their own entertainment. Nothing as fancy as a summer ball, just a normal Friday night pub crawl in Andover. Fridays and Saturdays are squaddie nights in Andover. Soldiers come into town from several camps in the vicinity and do some serious drinking. The pubs are full, the streets are packed with drunken revellers, and it's no place for pacifists, vegetarians or homosexuals.

Tonight Corporals Hitch, Lock, LeCornu, Rooney and Harrison are relying on a tried and trusted method to get large quantities of alcohol into the system as quickly and effectively as possible. They're playing spoof. Each of them puts a number of coins in their right hand – any number between nought and three. They then take it in turns to guess the total number of coins. The person who wins leaves the game. The rest carry on, repeating the process. Eventually there is one unfortunate person left, who is invited to buy everyone a round of drinks of the winner's choice. In this instance, Mark Hitch has decided they should all drink port and Marcus Lock has to pay for them. Within an hour the Town and Mills pub is completely out of port. Mark Hitch looks triumphant: 'It's time to move on...'

Back at the ball, Jenny has peaked and been taken to bed by her husband Steve. Andy is now on top of the mess bar, dancing and singing. He's taken off his jacket and is sporting a very sweaty T-shirt. Relations with Vanessa have become a little strained, because he's so busy being the clown prince that he's not paying her much attention. Andy knows he's behaving 'like a prat' but seems incapable of doing anything about it. His audience are egging him on, and he can't resist an audience. He tries to break-dance on the bar and, although it's impressive while it lasts, it doesn't last long. He falls to the floor. Fortunately alcohol is a great painkiller.

Outside, JP Miller is altogether more in control. He's on the bouncy castle, treating the girls to a display of double somersaults and back flips. He's had to take off his spurs to avoid puncturing the inflatable. Other officers are at the rifle range, demonstrating their shooting prowess and then blaming the sighting of the gun when they miss the target. They can also amuse themselves at a casino or on a full-scale bumper car ride. The Army certainly knows how to throw a good party.

In Andover the pubs have closed and the squaddie population seems to have moved *en masse* to Flicks Night Club. The place is teeming. It's hot, noisy and charged with testosterone. It's essentially a meat market; girls and boys are eyeing each other up, daring each other to make a move. But the corporals from Middle Wallop are more interested in drinking than coupling. They claim they can't stand the place, but they still end up here most Friday nights because it's the only venue where they can carry on drinking after hours. They refuse to dance until the DJ plays the latest UB40 number and then they move on to the packed floor as a group.

Jim LeCornu makes a half-hearted attempt to chat up a girl while he's dancing, but the rest of the corporals are either married (Harrison) or in long-term relationships (Hitch, Lock, Rooney). After a couple of dances they return to the bar and carry on drinking. Marcus Lock is particularly conscious of his behaviour at the moment. He's had a decision from the Regimental Sergeant Major on the vending machine incident at St Mawgans. He'll have to pay a £50 fine and make an apology. He thinks it's a harsh penalty but he's thankful that he's avoided the ultimate punishment, dismissal from the course. He's now trying to avoid anything that hints at trouble, for fear of blotting his copybook even further.

By two o'clock they call it a night and head back to the base, via the local kebab house. At about the same time, the officers at the mess are getting their second wind. A full English breakfast is being served, with bacon, eggs and fried bread to soak up the alcohol. Satisfactorily refuelled, they can go back to their bouncy castles and bumper cars and carry on partying.

By four o'clock most of the guests have gone home. By five o'clock the last stragglers are playing truth or dare. Most of the 'truth' questions involve details of people's sexual habits. Most of the 'dares' involve taking off items of clothing or kissing other people in the group. But then the challenges become more varied. JP is dared to climb to the top of the lamp-post, which he does with some relish, only to place the palm of his hand on a wasp's nest at the top. He shins down extremely quickly and rushes inside to run water over his hand. That's the end of his evening.

Finally, the most daring dare is offered – and accepted. A young officer from Course 355 has to climb to the top of the regimental flag pole and take his trousers down. With impressive co-ordination under the influence of alcohol, he shins his way up the pole. But no one has realized that it is made of plastic, and plastic bends. As he climbs higher, the pole starts to warp. His mates tell him to come down, but he's a driven man. He reaches the top – 50 feet up – and the pole is creaking. If it breaks he'll be seriously injured. But he's only interested in getting his trousers down and achieving the dare. By now the others are screaming for him to descend and he finally relents, slipping back to earth with his trousers hanging down around his ankles. He is applauded all the way back to his seat. But the flag pole – the same flag pole from which the Corps flag had been so reverently lowered earlier in the evening – is not in good shape. Instead of standing proud and priapic, it is drooping rather sadly; more a parabola than a straight line. The jollity of the stragglers is somewhat soured by the thought of how the President of the Mess Committee will react when he finds out.

Finally at six o'clock everyone has gone to bed, except Andy James. True to his word, he is the last one at the party. The sun has come up, the birds are singing and workmen are pulling down the marquee. But Andy is quietly pouring himself another drink:

> It's been a bloody bally-ho brilliant night. Bloody good crack. I know I've been a bit of a fool, but that's nothing new.... We have to chill out now, because when we come back from holidays we'll be starting Advanced Rotary, and what we've been doing until now has been a picnic compared to what we'll do on Advanced.... I know it will be hard work, but I'm looking forward to it.'

And, with that, Andy downs his last glass of wine, gets up and heads off to find Vanessa, who has gone to bed long ago.

Friday, 16 September

The summer holidays already seem like a distant memory. Andy went away with Vanessa. Jenny went on a trip to France and Spain with her husband. Mickey Rooney and Jim LeCornu spent two weeks together in Crete. Mark Hitch returned to his beloved Lake District. Wherever they went and whatever they did, they all benefited from the break. They had a whole month without thinking about helicopters.

But now they're back at Middle Wallop and for the last two and a half weeks they have been doing intensive revision, working on the weakest areas of their flying, trying to iron out problems in advance of today's Final Handling Test. It is the last rite of Basic Rotary.

Like any big exam the Final Handling Test – or FHT – is a cause of anxiety for the trainees. Everything seems to be riding on this one flight. To make matters worse, they aren't being assessed by their instructors any more but by examiners from Aviation Standards Wing. However, the ordeal is blown out of proportion. The FHT isn't designed to trip them up, so much as confirm that they've picked up all the prescribed skills over the past few months. Having got this far, it *should* be a formality, just as long as they all keep their nerve.

And so it proves. One by one they land and get the good news. JP Miller achieves the best pass; Jenny Firth and Mickey Rooney both felt they let themselves down after scoring highly in the sorties leading up to the FHT, but both passed; as did Marcus Lock and the other corporals. Marcus sums up the mood of the group: 'I was bloody nervous and didn't fly that well, but I passed and that's all that matters. It feels like a massive weight has been lifted.'

The only problem is a technical one. Andy James's communication system went down on his test, so his flight had to be aborted. He'll have to re-sit on Monday. It's an irritation, but at this stage nothing more. On Monday he'll pass and Basic Rotary will be over for Course 354.

Monday, 19 September

Monday comes and Andy doesn't pass. He re-sits the FHT but this time an element of doubt has entered his mind: 'what if...'. And the doubt gnaws away at his confidence. And he makes simple mistakes. And the doubt spreads. And more mistakes follow.

The holidays are over and it's back to work for Course 354.

And so on. It's a familiar enough pattern – a vicious cycle of self-induced pressure – and it has turned one of the most confident members of the course into a rattle of nerves.

Andy has now been placed on review. He's been given a new instructor and five more revision flights to prepare for a second re-sit FHT, which will be treated as a make-or-break check ride. His earlier comments about looking forward to Advanced Rotary are starting to sound decidedly premature. If he doesn't sort out his problems quickly, he won't even make it to next week. Andy is in a state of shock:

> It's never crossed my mind to consider going on review. Now I can't believe that I'm in a position where I'll soon have a ride which decides my whole future career. If you fail your driving test it's not a problem – you can do it again in a month. But fail your flying test and it is a big problem. You can't do it again a month later. It's bloody petrifying!

Tuesday, 27 September

'Frequency is inversely proportional to wavelength and can be shown by the formula: speed = frequency multiplied by wavelength. Therefore, as you increase frequency, wavelength decreases and vice versa.' Eight members of Course 354 are attending a lecture on electromagnetic warfare. They are busy scribbling notes, trying to keep up with the flow of gobbledigook. They are two days into a week of groundschool before Advanced Rotary. Judging by the look of utter bemusement on their faces, they are wondering how they'll survive the week, let alone the coming five months of Advanced Rotary.

The ninth member of the course is skipping class. Andy will have to catch up in his own time, when – or if – he survives today's flight. This is the re-sit of the re-sit and it will be supervised by the Chief Flying Instructor. For a week Andy has been alternately cosseted and cajoled by his new instructor. He has been going to bed early, studying hard and avoiding the bar. With great eloquence he describes the last seven days as 'a bloody nightmare'.

In the event, Andy flies a good FHT and the CFI passes him with a high green. After all the drama of Mark Finch's demise, there is something anti-climactic about the way Andy slips back

Each new phase is accompanied by more technical detail.

into the crewroom after the flight and finds no one from the course to share his joy. They're all too busy in the lecture hall learning electronics. Instead Andy goes outside for a 'celebratory fag'.

He is able to unwind at last and reflect on what he's been through. It's been a lesson in how pressure can take root. 'I was so nervous I'd jump into the helicopter at the start of each flight and need to go to the loo straight away. I kept getting things wrong I normally never get wrong.' But he is sanguine enough to think that the experience has probably been for the best. The shock of getting so close to failure will shake him up. He knows he'll have to work a lot harder if he's going to pass Advanced Rotary. He also knows he'll have to be *seen* to work a lot harder.

> People thought I was taking it easy, because I appear to have a casual approach. It's true I am casual in the mess, but when it comes to this I've never really been casual. Maybe I shouldn't be casual at all, and then people won't get the wrong impression.

It's lunchtime and Andy wanders over to the mess, to receive the congratulations of his peers. Outside, the flag pole has been restored to a fine, upright state after much forcible straightening. Inside, a group of young officers, including JP Miller, are sitting in armchairs reading newspapers. When Andy walks in, they seem genuinely relieved by the news and shake his hand. JP sometimes finds Andy a bit too *gash* for his tastes but, like the others, he'd have been sorry to lose the 'mess pet', their court jester. He teases him by suggesting it was a case of 'third time lucky'.

After lunch, Andy rejoins the rest of the course in the lecture room. By the end of the day, he gets more good news. Herbert, the cuddly hippo that he has had since childhood, was recently kidnapped by Marcus Lock and an anonymous ransom note was sent, along with a photo of it in a noose. Today Marcus has decided that the joke has run its natural course and he has returned the hippo to its grateful owner. Andy is entitled to feel that things are looking up.

Monday, 3 October

'Welcome to 670 Squadron. Congratulations on getting so far. What you're going to do here is face a whole load of new challenges. All I can say is rise to them.' It's the start of the Advanced Rotary phase of the training and the stakes have suddenly changed. Until now they have been taught civilian flying skills by civilian instructors. From today they become military pilots, members of 670 Squadron, and they're in the hands of military instructors. At the moment they're being addressed by their new Flight Commander, Captain Nick Wharmby. 'Every single one of you will have a problem on this phase, I promise you. And when it happens – I won't say if.... When it happens, be honest with yourself. Instructors will spot a bluffer at 100 yards.'

Nick Wharmby is the *wunderkind* of Middle Wallop. As a child he lived up the road from the base and cycled over to watch the helicopter display team. From that moment he decided he was going to become a helicopter pilot and nothing has stopped him. At nineteen he was awarded his commission. At twenty he became one of the youngest pilots to win his wings; at twenty-four, the youngest to qualify as an instructor; and now – at twenty-five – he's the youngest instructional flight commander at Middle Wallop. He has every reason to be apprehensive: in charge for the first time of nine trainees and a team of eight instructors, who are all older than him. But if he has any nerves, they don't show. Nick Wharmby is a young man with extraordinary self-confidence. Fresh-faced and good-looking, he's the epitome of the 'stable extrovert' that the Army deems to be the ideal character type for a successful pilot.

The nine faces watching and listening to Nick look like anything but the faces of stable extroverts. They are quiet and intense, rather fearful of what terrible treats Nick has in store for them. They've heard so much about this stage, they wouldn't be surprised to discover that their new instructors have horns concealed under their helmets and small pointed tails tucked into their flightsuits. Nick is trying not to disappoint them. He rattles through the syllabus to come: it's a jumble of acronyms – IF, NVG, FRASCA, AOP, Navex, Tacex, and so on – which seem a world away from the familiar territory of Basic Rotary. He tells them that they've been mothered until now and they're in for a culture shock. They'll be expected to show far more initiative from now on. 'You're all officers and NCOs – act like them. If you see that something needs doing, then do it. Don't come running to me. I'm busy enough.' By the time he's finished, his audience look dazed. He asks if there are any questions. There are none. He tells them not to look so worried. And then, when he can

Captain Nick Wharmby is Middle Wallop's boy wonder. He's the youngest person ever to become a flight commander.

keep up the tough guy image no longer, he smiles. 'Normally at this stage we say – just to allay your fears – "don't worry, we can't make you pregnant". But this time,' he says, looking at Jenny, 'I'd better not say it.' At last the trainees laugh. They've heard enough to know that laughs will be few and far between over the next weeks.

Tuesday, 4 October

The first of the acronyms to tackle is IF – it stands for Instrument Flying. So far they have been maintaining visual contact with the ground at all times. If the weather gets bad they don't take off or if they are caught in a storm they fly slower and lower and might even go to ground and sit it out. However, as military pilots operating on the battlefield, they can't afford to go slower or lower, let alone be forced to land. So they have to learn to fly through cloud and rain without any form of visual reference, using only their instruments, flying just as fast and confidently as if it were a nice sunny day.

The problem is that today *is* a nice sunny day. So they have to simulate low cloud conditions. This they do by blacking out the cockpit with a screen across the field of view of the right-hand seat pilot. The trainees then attach special blinkers to their helmets – they call them 'bat wings' – which are designed to cut out all other references and focus their vision exclusively on the instrument console. They take off from dispersal with the bat wings tucked up and out of the way. The instructor positions the aircraft clear of the circuit and then it's bat wings down and instruments only.

Marcus Lock is the first to try instrument flying. He's at 1000 feet, flying at 100 knots on a heading of 70 degrees. He knows this only because his instruments tell him so. As far as he's concerned he could be anywhere, but his instruments confirm he's on course, and the aim of the exercise is to place complete faith in the instruments. Because this is a training sortie, he also has an instructor sitting alongside him without bat wings, screen or any other impediment to his vision, double-checking that all is well. 'Another Gazelle at three o'clock, half a mile, not conflicting.' The instructor also acts as a safety lookout, watching for other aircraft in the skies. The words 'not conflicting' are what

Flying into cloud, the trainees have to rely on instruments only. They ignore what their brain is telling them and put complete trust in their dials.

the trainee wants to hear. It means his flight path is not destined to meet that of the other aircraft. If ever the instructor says 'conflicting', he has to take evasive action.

Marcus's instructor is Captain Simon Thorn, a young Australian pilot on an exchange visit to Middle Wallop. He's used to flying Hueys back home, so when he came here he had to do a conversion course on to the Gazelle. Now he loves it: 'It's like moving from an estate car to a sports car. It's kind of fun.' He'll be sad to leave Middle Wallop when his year runs out.

'OK Marcus, I want you to turn left on to a heading of zero eight zero degrees.' Marcus looks down at his compass and starts the turn, but this is where his faith in the instruments is tested. When turning, the brain relies on visual references to make sense of the move. Take away those references and the brain gets confused. His internal balance system thinks he's levelled out when the dials are telling him he's still turning. Which is he to believe, brain or dials?

'Marcus, hold it there. You've got to trust your AI, mate.' The AI is the altitude indicator, the most important of all the instruments. It sits in a bowl and provides an artificial horizon, giving a visual representation of the pitch and roll attitudes that the helicopter is flying at all times. When the two horizontal lines match up, and the spirit level is in the middle, it's in balance, flying efficiently. When they're out of kilter, it's straining to be brought back to the level again. The simple rule is: if the AI is happy, the helicopter is happy.

At the moment Marcus's AI is not happy. He has corrected his turn, but now he's over-compensated, with the result that he's out of balance and his speed has dropped. He's making the classic beginner's mistake of chasing the dials. After the flight he explains:

> It's all right if you concentrate on one instrument at a time, but it doesn't work like that. I mean I was looking at one instrument, trying to recognize what was happening with that one. And by the time I'd corrected that, the others were going. So I'd go to another one and try and correct that. But by the time I'd come back, the other one was gone. So, rather than looking at them all and going, OK, pull a bit of power, change my attitude and add a bit of pedal all at the same time, I was trying to do everything separately, and ended up fighting the aircraft.

Doing battle with the instruments from under cover of his bat wings, Marcus has the look of an intense man.

Down in the hangar, those who aren't flying are planning. The culture shock of Advanced Rotary is felt just as much on the ground as in the air. All the sorties have to be meticulously planned from now on by the trainees themselves. They're required to work out their routes, know the radio frequencies, liaise with air traffic control, check the weather reports, order up fuel, and do all the other things that their instructors did for them on Basic Rotary. They work from the flight planning room, a large room overlooking the dispersal area. This will be their mission control for the next few months.

At the moment there are maps everywhere. Andy James and Jim LeCornu are marking up their routes; Jenny is trying to work out the best way of folding her map so the relevant information will be easily accessible when she's flying; Mickey

Rooney is on the phone, using a large-scale map to discuss his route plan with the control tower. Mark Hitch is in an adjacent room, briefing his instructor with all the information he has accumulated for his forthcoming flight. On Advanced Rotary the trainees brief the instructors, not vice versa.

When Marcus appears in the planning room with bat wings and screen in hand, the rest of them stop what they're doing and grill him for information. What was it like? Where did you go? How did you do? Marcus breaks into a knowing smile: 'It's bloody weird... bloody weird.' He puts his helmet down on the table, wipes his brow and notices for the first time that his flightsuit is wringing wet. 'I've sweated buckets up there.'

Thursday, 6 October

These are long days for Course 354. They're being pushed through a physically and mentally demanding routine: early starts, two or three hours preparing for a morning flight, then an hour in the air; followed by a debrief, a quick lunch and two or three hours preparing for an afternoon flight; another hour in the air and another debrief. It's intense work, carried out under constant time pressure. They know this is a critical stage. Trainees who don't pick up IF quickly don't survive long on the course.

For Jim LeCornu, the biggest problem is the mental arithmetic. He's unusual among the corporals in that he has an O-level in mathematics – his only academic qualification – but it doesn't seem to have made much difference: 'On the ground it's not so hard but in the air it's horrendous – trying to do sums while you're flying. And sometimes you just go into overload and you miss something. But you can't afford to miss anything.'

Mickey Rooney concurs with Jim: 'You're trying to fly it accurately and do what air traffic are telling you and do what your instructor is telling you, and remember not to go below minimum height restrictions and things like that.... But hopefully we'll get there.'

For Jenny Firth, the problem is one of assertiveness. She needs to have a stronger presence in the cockpit. She has to be clearer and more decisive:

> I still find it easy to defer to the more experienced person. I say, 'Oh I'm about to call so and so to say such and such. That's right, isn't it?' Rather than having the confidence to just get on with the radio call and trust myself.

But the best comment of the day comes from Paul Stoneman. He lands at dispersal, walks into the planning room, packs the bat wings and screen into his pigeonhole and sums up his latest flight: 'My instructor says the Gazelle was called a Gazelle because it's meant to be sleek, fast and graceful. But in my hands he says it's more like a three-legged donkey with a whisky habit.' He then trudges off disconsolately to get his debrief.

Come nightfall there's no let up for Course 354. This evening they're night flying, which means a mass brief at six o'clock, half an hour off for a sandwich and a coffee, and then back into the planning room to prepare for another flight. They did some night flying on Basic Rotary, but this is different. Now that they're military pilots they have to learn to fly at night the military way, using night vision goggles (or NVG, the next fearsome acronym).

The goggles are image-intensifying binoculars, as worn by the deranged serial killer in *Silence of the Lambs*. At the moment Andy James is in the planning room, trying to fit them to his helmet, looking anything but deranged. In fact he seems rather calm. He has recovered some of his composure since the scare at the end of Basic Rotary and, compared to some of the others, he has found the first days of instrument flying quite manageable. He's benefited from being assigned as Nick Wharmby's trainee. The two of them like each other, perhaps because Nick recognizes something of himself in Andy – that same simple joy in all things connected with flying.

'You idiot,' says Nick as he walks into the planning room and sees his trainee fiddling with the goggles. 'You've got them the wrong way round.' Andy suddenly looks less calm. 'I knew that, I knew that,' he insists and sets about swapping them over.

Nick leads Andy outside and helps him adjust the goggles so they fit properly over his eyes. 'OK, now turn them on.' Andy flicks a switch and gasps. 'Bloody hell... it's... it's... amazing.'

Andy is struggling for words to describe what he's seeing. All that was once dark is now light. The optics in the goggles are drawing on every scrap of luminance in the vicinity and enhancing them to create a wonderfully clear picture of the airfield. But because of the way the light is reflected, the image is a monochrome green. Andy lifts up his helmet to take his eyes away from the goggles. He can see nothing except some red navigation lights on Danebury Hillfort. He pulls the goggles back and the lights turn green, and everything comes into sharp focus. He can see the contours of the horizon dropping down from the hillfort, the sky is a light green, the hills are dark green. He can see a green car driving off in the distance. And to the right there is a ploughed field, showing up as lots of different shades of green. Andy is enjoying his new green world.

Now the hard bit – flying with the goggles on. They take off as normal, using a landing lamp to fly by. Then they get to a goggling up point and 'go green'. Nick starts by demonstrating to Andy the pitfalls of flying NVG: the problem of burn out when the goggles are pointed at bright light sources, like car headlights; the difficulty of judging height, depth and distance; and the complexity of map-reading when nothing is quite what it seems.

'See that road down there?' asks Nick.

'What the small one, by the farmhouse?'

'Yeah. What road is that?'

'The B3084?' Andy offers hopefully.

'Nope. It's actually a river.... With NVG they look the same from up here.'

Nick flies Andy down to low-level territory on Salisbury Plain, and invites him to take over and practise a hover. By now Andy has had so many hours hovering, he can do it without thinking. But in the dark, using the goggles, he has suddenly lost all his peripheral vision, and he's having to work really hard just to judge his position relative to the ground. When he manages it and steadies the aircraft, Nick congratulates him and by way of a reward suggests he takes another look under the goggles. 'Aagh... you can't see shagall!' Andy switches back to the goggles. 'You won't catch me again trying to fly under 200 feet without these on, no way!' Nick takes over control, laughs and feels that the lesson has been learnt.

After an hour in the air they fly back to base, with Nick telling Andy stories about using NVG in Northern Ireland: how they'd go on night patrols in the border area, drop off troops, and pick them up again without ever being visible to the naked eye. All any passer-by would hear was the whirr of the rotor blades, but they'd never know where the sound was coming from.

Back in the planning room, everyone is comparing notes about their first experience of NVG. Some enjoyed it more than others. The general consensus is that it was 'spooky'. The only person who can't share in the excitement is Mickey Rooney. All evening, he's had a face on him like thunder. He heard today that his girlfriend, who's stationed at the Air Corps base at Dishforth in Yorkshire, has chucked him for someone else on the base. For this evening at least, the irrepressibly cheerful Mickey Rooney is inconsolable. It's a reminder to them all how difficult it is to make relationships work on such an intense course, particularly when they're being conducted over such long distances.

By the time the last flights are over and the helicopters have been wheeled back into the hangar, it has gone midnight. They've been working on and off for sixteen hours and they're exhausted, but no one's going to get to sleep in a hurry. The effect of NVG is to send the eyes popping and the brain spinning. Nick recommends a medicinal whisky or two.

He recognizes the stress they must all be feeling; it's the stress of being bombarded with new information and new skills, and having to learn them at a pace dictated by the system not the individual. He's sympathetic to their plight, but he thinks it is a good way to teach them: 'We throw them in at the deep end when they get up here and see if they sink or swim.' After all they're meant to be military pilots, and if they can't cope with pressure at this stage, what will they be like on a battlefield? Nick returns to his room in the Mess, opens a bottle of whisky, and helps himself to a dose of his own medicine.

Friday, 7 October

'I'm bolloxed, to tell you the truth.' The pressure of the first week has taken its toll on Marcus Lock. After yesterday's night-flying sortie he was back on instrument flying again this morning and had a poor flight. His instructor Simon Thorn scored it a red (a failure). He picked Marcus up for his division of attention and awareness:

> He should be using about 80 per cent of his brain to fly the aircraft, leaving some spare capacity to think about the instructions being given to him by air traffic control and where he is in time and space. But unfortunately Corporal Lock is working toward using 100 per cent to fly the aircraft and there's very little spare to appreciate what's happening around him.

Marcus has a simpler explanation: 'I didn't get to bed until one.... I was just knackered.' Sitting in the crewroom, quietly shaking his head at the injustice of it all, Marcus looks fed up with the world. 'I'll be glad to get away from this place, because I'm not spending the weekend here. No way.'

It was inevitable that the strain of the new workload was going to show sooner or later. The only surprise is that it has happened sooner rather than later; this is only the fourth day of IF. Marcus is as surprised as anyone else. He did well on Basic Fixed Wing, survived aero-medical training, had some problems on Basic Rotary, but came through them all to get a reasonable pass on his FHT. He works hard and is highly motivated – partly because he knows what the alternative holds: digging trenches in the Infantry.

But perhaps it shouldn't be such a surprise. Marcus is a mercurial character, as evidenced by his problems at St Mawgan. When he's up, he's very up. He got more of a kick from the early days of rotary training than anyone else on the course. He thought it was all 'absolutely brilliant'. But when things go wrong for him he has a tendency to fly off the handle – often at himself. His instructors are forever picking him up on his habit of telling himself off in mid-flight. It is not unusual for a trainee to be self-critical, but in Marcus's case it seems pathological. He gets frustrated too quickly and allows his confidence to drop. His performance then suffers, he blames himself further, and the confidence drops further. He's not sure how to arrest the decline before it slips into freefall. 'I know I always put myself down, but that's just the way I am. I can't do anything abut it.'

Having failed today's flight, Marcus is summoned for a chat

with the Flight Commander. Nick is a little uncertain how to handle the situation; this is the first time he's had to put anyone on review. But, after some deliberation, he decides it's best to keep it casual. He carefully positions himself on the edge of the desk with an air of measured informality and then calls Marcus in. He breaks the news as gently as possible:

'Right, it hasn't been going as well as it might have been, Corporal Lock.'

'Right, Sir.'

'I've been speaking to Captain Thorn and we've given you until the end of the week to sort out the few problems you've been having.'

OK, Sir.'

'What we're going to do now is give you five extra hours to get you back on line. All right? Are you happy with that? Or as happy as you can be?'

'Yes, Sir.' Marcus tries to sound sanguine.

'You've got five hours now. That's a lot of flying time.... Any questions?'

'No, Sir.'

Nick gives him a well-practised smile, and sends him on his way. 'Good luck, Corporal Lock.' Marcus scuttles out of the office, and Nick looks rather pleased with the way he's handled the exchange. He decides it was definitely a good move to sit on the edge of the desk, much more human.

Warming to his role as disciplinarian, Nick tells the group he would like to talk to them before they head off for the weekend. He gathers them together in the main briefing room and has a 'quick word about course spirit':

> We haven't seen any! Last night's duty student didn't get to bed until half-past one, because he was on one of the later night-flying slots. Yet there were four people who could quite easily have got hold of the programmes and sorted it out. Corporal LeCornu was poring over a map, having a few problems with planning. How many of you helped him?... Exactly. Think about it over the weekend. You're all in this together; you're not just nine individuals.

Nick gives them a long hard stare and walks out of the briefing room, leaving behind nine stunned faces.

It's been quite a week for Course 354. Not only have they

started Advanced Rotary, and been introduced to the rigours of IF and NVG, they've also seen one of their number go on review, and have now received a reprimand for their lack of team spirit. If that was week one, what will week two be like? The weekend break could not have come at a better time.

Monday, 10 October

Marcus is under his bat wings, focusing his gaze on the dials. He is flying the first of his five review flights with a new instructor, Warrant Officer Alan Arnold, one of 670 Squadron's IF specialists. He'll fly one sortie a day for the whole week and then his progress will be judged. He doesn't have a clear goal to achieve – such as going solo – but he knows he's expected to show significant signs of progress by the end of the week. Put simply, he'll need to start scoring blues and greens rather than browns and reds.

Although the situation is serious, review doesn't carry quite the same fear as it once did. There have now been several people on review, and only one of them – Mark Finch – ended up getting chopped. Mark Hitch survived on Fixed Wing; Marcus himself spent a short time on review towards the beginning of Basic Rotary (ironically, as a result of a personality clash with his instructor); Jim LeCornu experienced two spells of review during Basic Rotary; and Andy James overcame his problems only two weeks ago. The instructors are always telling them not to worry so much about review, to see it as bonus training rather than the first step to the chop. Many of the instructors themselves went on review as trainees and they all managed to come out with their wings, so there's nothing to fear.

Marcus is trying hard to bear this in mind and think positively as he scans the instrument console. He spent the weekend in Canterbury with his fiancée Angela, and he's returned in good spirits, determined to curb his self-destructive tendencies and pull himself through this patch: 'It's not going to be easy – the stress factor's just gone up about 110 per cent – but I know I've got to relax more.... If I can just relax, I'll be all right.'

This first review flight is a LARS sortie. Another flight, another acronym: LARS stands for Lower Airspace Radar

Service. Marcus has to make an approach to the airfield at Boscombe Down, flying by instruments all the way, and guided in by the radar operators at the airfield. It's one of the tougher instrument flying sorties in the syllabus, and a good test of his ability.

The problem with LARS is that the trainees are being watched and directed all the time. Marcus is picked up on the Boscombe Down radar when he's 8 miles from the base and is talked through every step of his landing. On the screens the air traffic controllers have an optimal path of approach – the glide path – and they are trying to get Marcus to fly as close to that line as possible. They issue a stream of directions and adjustments: 'Turn left 20 degrees on to a heading of 270.... Right 3 degrees.... On centre-line.... Descending too fast.... Check speed.... Now you're left of centre-line.' The accuracy demanded by the air traffic controllers is unforgiving; Marcus feels as if he's having to fly like a 'bloody autopilot'.

The rest of the course are in the flight planning room, marking up routes and planning their briefs. They're so busy with their own flying, they haven't much time to think about Marcus. For the most part they're sympathetic, but not unduly concerned. Andy's reaction is typical: 'I know what it's like for him. It's horrible being on review, no two ways about it. But he'll be all right. I mean, everyone's having teething problems at this stage.... These are early days still.'

Of greater concern at the moment is the ticking off they got from Nick on Friday. They've always prided themselves on how well they get on, so they're surprised – and a little hurt – to be criticized in such stark terms. Mickey Rooney presents the case for the defence: 'I don't think our course spirit's that bad. OK we bug each other every now and again, but I think we sort of pull together when it matters.' The others are inclined to concur with Mickey, but they recognize that things have probably slipped since they started Advanced Rotary. As Jim LeCornu puts it: 'It's possible that we've all been a bit overawed by this phase and we've gone our separate ways. But now is the time to pull together and sort things out.' Andy agrees. Over the last week he's become so close to Nick that he's starting to sound like his official spokesman: 'I wasn't surprised by what he said. It needed somebody at this stage to

come in and say, "You lot – get a grip, sort your lives out or you're going to fall apart." I'm glad he's done it.'

Whatever the rights and wrongs of Nick's reprimand, it has certainly had the desired effect of getting them to think more about the group dynamics. He's seen the pattern before: people arrive at Advanced Rotary and get so bogged down in the new workload that they

Marcus Lock is flying blind. He's relying on the air traffic controllers at Boscombe Down to watch his every move and guide him down safely. There is no margin for error.

focus in on their own problems, rather than looking after each other. He's convinced that the secret to surviving the course is team spirit. Team spirit builds confidence, and confidence is such a powerful factor it can pull trainees of average ability through even the toughest of hurdles.

As a contribution to the process of team-building, the instructors have suggested that everyone – instructors and trainees – goes out for a social night next Wednesday. Their preference is for a night at the local go-karting circuit – a chance for all the pilots to burn some rubber. But the suggestion meets with a mixed response. The three officers on the course reckon it is a brilliant idea and sign up straight away. But the corporals think that, at £27 per head, it's too expensive and they're threatening to boycott the evening. Nick is none too impressed. This isn't quite the show of course spirit he was hoping to engender. Captain Sean Dufosee, one of the instructors on Advanced Rotary, has been given the unenviable task of negotiating between the officers and corporals.

While the go-karting debate goes on, Marcus slips back into the crewroom and helps himself to a coffee. From his face it's obvious that the flight hasn't gone particularly well – it's been scored 'brown' (below average). A couple of the others try and cheer him up, but then they have to hurry off and brief their instructors about their next sorties. Marcus takes another sip of coffee and sits down. He's starting to look like a worried man.

Friday, 14 October

It's the end of the second week on Advanced Rotary. People are coming down from their flights, packing away their gear, changing out of their flying suits and heading off base as quickly as possible.

By the time Marcus Lock enters the flight planning room it's all but empty. He signs off his aircraft, folds up his bat wings and packs his bag. Nothing's been confirmed yet, but he suspects that he's just flown his last flight on the course. That was his fifth and final review flight, a check ride supervised by Nick Wharmby and, like the others, it was littered with basic mistakes of awareness and division of attention; it has been scored 'red'. IF is a specific skill and, like riding a bike, it comes eventually. But Marcus has run out of time to keep learning.

Nick consoles Marcus by telling him there's still hope. The Chief Flying Instructor and the Commandant could take a number of decisions. They could give him anything up to another five hours of review to help him crack IF, or they could give him some time off and let him start Advanced Rotary all over again on the next course. But Marcus knows better. He remembers being in the same position, trying to reassure Mark Finch after his last flight, and giving unconvincing assurances that there was still hope of a reprieve. Marcus knows what happened to Mark Finch, and he knows that he can expect the same treatment. He's already resigned himself to the prospect of being chopped. 'Everyone struggles on something on this course and the instrument flying was my thing... I just couldn't do it. Oh well, life's a bitch.'

One thing is certain, Marcus will have a stay of execution until Monday morning. The check ride has finished so late in the day that there isn't time for the necessary discussions to take place.

Monday, 17 October

It's eight o'clock and Marcus is in the corridor waiting to be called into the CFI's office. He looks surprisingly cheerful for a man about to be chopped. He says it's just a cover: 'I'm very good at putting up shields.' But there is another explanation. He has spent the weekend with Angela and she's helped him hatch a new plan. He's going to apply for a transfer to the Army Air Corps, not as a pilot, but as an aircrewman, or failing that as a groundcrewman. He's decided that if he can't fly helicopters he can do the next best thing and work with the people who fly them. That way he can still enjoy helicopters without having the stress of being a pilot.

The CFI gives him the nod and Marcus Lock marches into the office. He salutes and takes a seat. Behind the desk sits Colonel Wawn, the Commandant. He's consulted with the CFI and they've made a decision. He doesn't take long to break the news:

'I'm sorry to have to tell you, Corporal Lock, but I've decided to suspend you from flying training.'

'OK, Sir.' Marcus looks quite cheerful about the news.

'Now you merit an explanation...' The Commandant goes into a lengthy résumé of the problems Marcus has experienced on the course. He ends by asking Marcus whether he acknowledges these problems and feels he's been fairly treated.

'Yes, Sir. All the instructors have been excellent.'

Colonel Wawn changes tack. 'What I want you to do now is go away, come to terms with it and then think about what you'd like to do...'

'I've already thought about it, Sir.'

'What? Do tell us?'

'I want to transfer to the Air Corps, Sir.'

'Aah yes... tricky.'

'I don't mind being on the ground side. I've seen what the Air Corps does and how it operates and I want to transfer. It was always the second option in the back of my mind, if I failed the course.'

'Hmm.... Well, we'll see what we can do. I'll talk tothe Manning and records office and let you know.'

Marcus leaves the meeting and heads back to the crewroom. He has just been chopped, but he's more interested in telling everyone about his transfer. They're not sure whether to commiserate or congratulate him. Marcus suggests that, with a bit of luck, they'll all be working together soon; him as a crewman, them as pilots.

Unfortunately all the talk of transfer is somewhat premature. In the flourish with which he presented his request to the Commandant, Marcus didn't really listen to the response. More specifically, he didn't listen to the tone of the response. When Colonel Wawn said 'we'll see what we can do', Marcus took it as meaning 'leave it to me and we'll see what we can do'. In reality it meant, 'Don't hold your breath, but we'll see what we can do.' The Commandant was trying to dampen his hopes. He suspected, from the moment Lock made the suggestion, that this was a slightly desperate 'rebound' measure, by someone trying to salvage something positive out of failure. The chances of the transfer being granted are very remote.

In the crewroom, Marcus is still fantasizing about life as a crewman: 'Maybe I'll be able to jump into the front seat every now and then, and even if I can't wazz it around on my own, being wazzed around by somebody else will be almost as good.' Everyone else – from Nick downwards – agrees it is a great idea, and wishes Marcus the best of luck in his new venture.

Wednesday, 19 October

It's the date of the much-debated social night. The corporals have dug their heels in and refused to sign up for the go-karting. The best they'll offer is to meet the officers and instructors for a drink in the pub afterwards. In the name of harmony, Sean Dufosee has backed down and changed the plans. Go-karting has been cancelled, and a cheaper alternative has been proposed and accepted. Course 354 are going bowling.

Crash, bang, wallop. The skittles are flying. Mickey Rooney accepts the applause of the others for the first strike of the evening. Jim LeCornu is cursing his luck that he keeps leaving one or two skittles standing. Andy James is so busy having conversations with just about everyone in the group, he forgets to take his turn. Jenny Firth wanders up diffidently and rolls the ball very slowly but, much to everyone's surprise, she registers the second strike of the evening. By contrast, JP Miller delivers the ball with great pace and technique, but lands it way off target. Mark Hitch studies the skittles intensely, as if locked in mortal combat with them. Is it too fanciful to suggest that their different bowling styles give a clue to the way the trainees fly?

There is a strange mood at Breakers bowling alley. Everyone's trying hard to enjoy themselves. They're also conscious that they're meant to be team-building, but they're without one of the key members of the team. Marcus has already left Middle Wallop on leave and the others are coming to terms with his absence. Jenny sums up their feelings: 'It's going to hit us a lot harder than it did with Staff Finch because we've all been together that much longer and developed stronger bonds. It feels a bit like a period of mourning.' Andy is shocked by the speed of Marcus's departure: 'It all happened so quickly... I went home on Friday afternoon not knowing how his check ride went, assuming it was OK. And then to come in on Monday and find that he'd been sacked was a big shock.' Mickey takes a more hard-headed attitude: 'It's a big shame, he

Jim LeCornu is used to being on review. He experienced it twice on Basic Rotary, and survived both times. Will it be third time unlucky?

was a nice guy – still is, I suppose – but we can't spend too much time moping about. We're here to get wings for ourselves, we've got to crack on.'

The most uneasy member of the group is Jim LeCornu. Last week, while Marcus was flying his last flights, Jim also went on review. It wasn't such a big deal for him; he has already been on review twice during Basic Rotary and both times managed to raise his performance at the right moment and do just enough to get by. Now that he's on review on Advanced Rotary, he's expecting to squeeze through again. But seeing Marcus go has worried him: 'No one was prepared for him to go, so it's woken us all up. You can't help thinking "who'll be next?". I always assumed he was doing better then me.' Jim's problems are very similar to Marcus's: his division of attention and awareness are poor. 'I find flying a helicopter accurately quite difficult enough, but being asked to do other things at the same time can send me into a frenzy and then I fall to pieces.' It is turning into a test of nerves – and patience.

Jim should have flown his fifth and final review flight today, but it was called off because of the weather. All being well, he'll fly it tomorrow, and – assuming he passes – some semblance of normality will return to the course. Jim hopes it might even grow stronger as a result of these problems:

> Marcus leaving can have one of two effects: either it will drag the course apart or pull it together. And – provided everyone else gets through the IF phase – I think it will be better for the course as it'll bring us closer together, definitely.

The bowling competition has ended and the scores have been totted up. Sean Dufosee, as master of ceremonies, announces the results. Somehow Andy James has come out as champion bowler, despite missing a turn. Andy excepts the groans of mock indignation with a theatrical bow. He's unrecognizable from the Andy James on review only three weeks ago. The old assurance and enthusiasm have definitely returned; suddenly he can do no wrong. It proves once again how quickly confidence can ebb and flow on this course.

Thursday, 20 October

Against expectations, Jim LeCornu fails his final review flight. This time he has been unable to show the progress demanded of him and he becomes the second casualty of the week.

But the CFI and Commandant decide that Jim has the ability to earn another crack at the course. Rather than return him to his old job as a groundcrewman, they will send him on aircrewman training, allow him two years' experience on Lynx and then, all being well, give him another place on the pilot's course sometime in 1996.

By contrast, they have decided to turn down Marcus Lock's request for a transfer to the Army Air Corps. He didn't have the qualifications to be considered as a groundcrewman and at his age – 28 – he would be hard-pressed to pick them up. To have taken him into the Corps and taught him from scratch would have meant making an exception of him, which they were unwilling to do, when they have plenty of younger, better qualified soldiers to choose from. Marcus Lock will now return to the Light Infantry and pick up his career where he left off. His request for a British posting, to be close to his fiancée, has also been turned down. The Light Infantry want him to rejoin his batallion at Paderborn in Germany.

Course 354 are not yet three weeks into Advanced Rotary, but only seven of the original ten members remain. These seven know that the hardest three and a half months of the training still lie ahead of them. At the present rate of progress, they are starting to wonder how many of them – if any – will make it to the Wings Parade in February. In the officers' mess bar there is a plaque commemorating the plight of Course 227, the only course so far which had to be aborted because all its members were chopped. Everyone on 354 is hoping that there won't be a need for a second plaque to be erected, one that reads 'R.I.P. Course 354: they came, they tried and they failed'.

Chapter Five

Under Pressure

Tuesday, 29 November

Salisbury Plain, Wiltshire

The red flag is flying on Salisbury Plain. It is a warning to the general public: keep out, live firing on the range. Hidden under a camouflage net – far from the public gaze – is a temporary artillery battery. A soldier dressed in full combat gear is standing by his field telephone. When he hears the command – 'Fire!' – he passes it on to the men operating the gun. The soldier in the jump seat does the honours: he pulls the firing lever and boom! A high explosive shell leaves the barrel of a 105mm gun at something approximating 10 000 miles per hour. The noise is loud enough to wake the dead, but none of the gunners even flinch. They're used to it.

About 10 miles away, Lieutenant JP Miller is sitting in a helicopter watching the target area. He's in radio contact with the artillery battery. He hears the word 'splash' and it's a signal that the shell is about to land. JP scans the horizon looking for any sign of smoke. 'There... between the two ridge lines.' The shell has missed its target by 200 yards. JP gets on the radio and calls for an adjustment in the gun's heading.

Course 354 are getting their first whiff of cordite. They've been working so hard on honing their flying skills, they've almost forgotten what they're in the Army for. Now they are getting a sharp reminder. Today they have an enemy to destroy and the firepower on hand to do so. Their job is to act as a pair of eyes for the artillery: to spot the target, relay information and watch as the shells explode. It sounds easy, but it isn't. It involves a combination of tactics, map-reading and radio communication skills. For the first time they're having to think about the realities of combat and entertain the notion of being both hunter and prey.

There are other changes too. The trainees have moved into the left-hand seat, the captain's seat. They're no longer flying – that's the instructor's job – now they are commanding the helicopter. They're directing the instructors where to fly and the gunners where to fire. Now they are in the final three months of the course, they'll be doing less flying and more captaincy. 'We're not making pilots any more. We're making potential aircraft commanders.' Nick Wharmby's words echo through Salisbury Plain.

JP Miller has had few difficulties so far. With a degree in pure mathematics and being the only graduate on the course, he probably has an advantage when it comes to academic discipline. But he's conscious that today's sortie will expose his biggest weakness – being in too much of a hurry. 'I think so far ahead of myself that I don't concentrate on what's at hand at the moment. Everything's happening so quickly, but in your mind it has to be quite clear, slow and logically thought through.'

JP's target is the hulk of a burnt-out tank sitting somewhere in the middle of the kill zone. It's up to JP to direct the shells right on to the hulk and furnish it with even more battle scars. But at the same time he must keep out of sight of the enemy, to avoid becoming a potential target himself. Accordingly, the helicopter remains below the horizon, popping up only to work out grid references, calculate the lie of the land and the direction of the wind. JP has to make his assessments as quickly as possible and then retreat back down below the skyline.

He's at a vantage point fully 2 miles from the target. The only way he can see what's going on is by using the Gazelle Observation Aid, the helicopter equivalent of a periscope. Equipped with powerful gyro-stabilized optics and 10:1 magnification, the GOA gives a remarkably clear view of the target. But establishing a proper grid reference is still an inexact science. The GOA was

The trainees are on the battlefield for the first time. They have to find a vantage point where they can see the enemy without being seen themselves.

originally designed by the British firm Ferranti to operate with a laser designating system creating a precise electronic lock on the target. But, for reasons of cost, the Army Air Corps chose not to equip their Gazelles with the laser facility. Nor will they ever do so. With the new attack helicopters on the way, the whole role of helicopters as an artillery observation post will change. The attack helicopters will carry their own battery of missiles and rockets, and need not involve a separate artillery unit. They will have the ability to destroy the enemy themselves.

But that is still in the future. For the moment JP is cursing the lack of laser precision on the GOA. He needs to rely instead on his own estimates. It means yet another juggling act: not with the collective, cyclic and pedals this time; but with the GOA, radio and map. In addition, he has the pressure of knowing his every move is being scrutinized by the instructor and a specialist artillery officer in the back seat. This pressure of being examined isn't new, it's just relentless. 'Every time you go up for a trip it's like going for a driving test. Most people do one maybe two driving tests in their lives. We do anything up to three driving tests a day.'

Confident of the enemy's position, JP signals for his instructor to dip below the horizon once more while he radios the grid reference to the artillery battery. His message is received 10 miles away, at a makeshift communications post hidden among the trees. They then convert the reference into coordinates and an angle of elevation relevant to the guns. This conversion, thankfully, is done electronically and the information is passed on to the gunners by field telephone. JP waits, with some trepidation, still hovering below the horizon. If he's got it wrong, then they'll get it wrong and the shell will miss the target.

Ten seconds later the radio crackles back into life. 'Splash!' JP cues his instructor to climb and see the danger area. Another miss. The previous shell landed 200 yards left of the target; this one lands 200 yards to the right. JP is disappointed, but at least he now has two good markers. If they can land the next shell between the first and second, he'll be right on target. He takes another look through the GOA, directs his instructor to drop down below the horizon and makes contact again with the artillery. The same process is repeated. Only this time when he hears 'splash' and pops up, he sees the shell land right by the tank. JP is delighted: 'Wow, dead on. One tank destroyed.' And then he adds, for good measure, 'Two other tanks on the run, enemy is retreating.' For JP at least, this is the real thing. His enemy may have been remarkably static and pliant – a sitting duck, in fact – but it was an enemy nevertheless and it has been dispatched lethally and efficiently. JP looks quietly pleased with himself.

Back in the bunker, Nick Wharmby is also pleased with JP. He compliments him on a good mission. His only criticism is of his radio skills. He should have changed frequency at one point, to receive a clearer signal from the artillery battery. JP takes the criticism in good part and cheerfully admits that he's 'totally incompetent' on the radio. Of all the skills he has yet to master, it's safe to assume this won't be the most difficult.

Next on the battlefield is Mark Hitch. Mark's morale has taken a dip recently, particularly since the departure of Marcus Lock and Jim LeCornu. While their failure so early in Advanced Rotary was a shock to everyone on Course 354, it was an extra blow to Mark. From day one he and Marcus shared a flat in Hotspur House and became firm friends. 'That Friday night when we started – 700 years ago – he came in with a bottle of Southern Comfort and we promised to help each other through all this. And he did – he helped me out of a lot of scrapes.' He's reminded again of his own vulnerability. 'It's stamped a message home to everyone else that no one is immortal. Since losing Staff Finch, we honestly thought we were going to get through with everyone, and then for Marcus and Jim to go...'

Mark Hitch is clearly not enjoying himself at the moment. His commitment to the Army is not in question; it has been evident from day one that he loves Army life. But each stage of the pilot's course has forced him into new challenges and new responsibilities. It's not quite the safe, confined world he has been used to during his six years as a groundcrewman. Then, he knew what each day would bring. Now, every day brings change and Mark is suspicious of change. He joined the Army for security and a job with a clearly defined career path, where promotion is the reward for hard work. He's already won his first two stripes. Now he wants to be a sergeant, and eventually work his way up to the rank of sergeant-major. Set against this ambition, the pilot's course seems too random. Here rank is not important; what matters is flexibility and initiative. Mark is having difficulty with both.

He doesn't perform well on his artillery observation exercise. His instructor keeps picking him up for basic mistakes: 'You're staying in sight of the enemy too long.... You're not talking to me enough.... You're not using me as your pilot.... You need to be more precise on the radio.... You've got to keep one step ahead of the aircraft.' Mark hates being watched and criticized – the driving test syndrome – and he is beginning to find the strain unbearable. Every time he looks over his shoulder, he sees an instructor watching him. There is no escape from helicopters. Life on the course is totally claustrophobic.

One recent anecdote about Mark Hitch sums up his mood. A couple of days ago a visiting Canadian officer was being taken for a courtesy flight around Middle Wallop. As is customary on such rides, the guest was given a chance to take control himself, just to see how difficult it is to hold a hover. He promptly let go of everything and allowed the rear of the Gazelle fuselage to come crashing into the turf. The Canadian escaped with minor injuries, the instructor was more seriously hurt and the Gazelle was a write-off. All in all, it was an expensive and embarrassing mistake.

The members of Course 354 were on the base at the time, and when they heard the news they were taken over to see the crash site. They were naturally curious to see for themselves what a crashed helicopter looks like, especially after spending so much time talking about emergency procedures and escape drills. But one of the course couldn't bear to join in the forensic examination. Mark Hitch was repelled by the entire incident. Already under pressure, the last thing he wanted to be reminded of was that helicopters have a habit of crashing.

Monday, 5 December

Middle Wallop, Hampshire

The Gazelles take off from Middle Wallop at fifteen-minute intervals. Into a hover, taxi to the spots and away. But this is no ordinary sortie. It is clear from the amount of luggage and equipment packed into the back seat of the Gazelle that they're off on a major journey.

They're heading north-west, over rolling English countryside, all neat fields and hedgerows. The first sign of change comes with the Severn River. Once they cross this barrier, the scenery changes. The hills get steeper, the grass scarcer, the rocks more prominent. The weather changes too. Middle Wallop was bathed in sunshine when they left, but now the sky is a blanket of alto-stratus cloud. They fly on. One valley after another – they all look so similar from the air. They are constantly crossing invisible borders of air traffic zones, changing frequencies and clocking in with new control towers as they go.

After two hours they make contact with the tower at RAE Llanbedr. This will be their base for the next three days, here on the edge of Snowdonia, ten minutes flying time from the MFTA, the mountain flying training area for all military aircraft. This is one of the most inhospitable and demanding terrains any helicopter can fly in.

'Make a southerly final approach into wind... wind now blowing 35 knots, gusting 45.'

The tower is calling down the first helicopter, being piloted by JP. The wind is a good 20 knots stronger than anything he's been used to at Middle Wallop. It's a matter of making an orbit of the landing site, getting a clear picture of the approach and hover taxiing in, ever so slowly. The Welsh groundcrewman is getting anxious. He's used to marshalling aircraft in such winds, but in this case he knows the pilot is a trainee and unfamiliar with the routine.

He need not have worried. JP's landing is fine, followed fifteen minutes later by Mickey Rooney. They've all been taught well enough to adapt their technique to the new conditions. Jenny is the next to materialize through the low-level cloud clinging to the horizon. She has more of a problem. She shoots her approach too fast, and finds she's out of limits for turning and taxiing. She goes round and tries again. This time she slows down and makes a successful landing, eventually ending up next to Mickey's helicopter. Afterwards, she is honest in her assessment of the flight. She knows it didn't go well. Aside from the final approach, she had problems all the way through, caused by poor map-reading: 'I found my way here, but probably not in the approved manner. I think we'll put that one down to experience and move on.'

As they arrive, the trainees set up their crewroom in one half of a distinctly uninspiring portacabin. The kettle goes on, the lunch boxes are opened, and they excitedly discuss the journey. JP tries out a well-prepared joke: 'When I came across the River Severn I was looking out for all these w(h)ales, but I couldn't see any.... Lots of sea, but no w(h)ales.' Nobody laughs. Undaunted, JP waits for another pause in the conversation and repeats it. Still not a snigger. Perhaps the sense of humour is different in Zimbabwe.

Half an hour after everyone else has arrived, Mark Hitch walks quietly into the portacabin. He was the second pilot to leave Middle Wallop, but he's the last to reach Llanbedr. He takes some gentle ribbing from his mates: he flew at the wrong speed, got lost a couple of times and misjudged his approach. JP tries his joke out on him, and Mark humours him by pulling a half-smile. He's trying not to dwell on his

The journey up to Snowdonia is a culture shock. The trainees have to swap the gentility of the English countryside for the rugged physicality of the mountain range.

flying problems. For the time being, he's happy just to be away from Middle Wallop. He pours himself a cup of coffee and joins in the banter.

On the other side of the portacabin the atmosphere is less upbeat. This is the instructors' crewroom, a thin dividing wall away from the trainees. Nick Wharmby is debriefing his instructors about the flights up here. Captain Simon Thorn, the Australian, expresses his general worries about Jenny and particularly her map-reading and lack of assertion in the cockpit. He knows that these few days in the mountains will be a challenge for her, and he'll be watching her closely. But at this stage he's optimistic that she'll rise to the challenge.

Less optimistic is the prognosis on Hitch. 'It's snowballing, it really is. He's just not aware of what's going on.... His loss procedure was hopeless. His approach here was much too fast. He's dangerous...' Sean Dufosee, Mark's instructor, is frustrated more than angry. He rates Mark's general handling, but he can't understand why his captaincy is so poor. 'He's absolutely closed in. Getting him to talk about anything in the air is a nightmare. Whether it's what he did at the weekend, to offering him a mint, he just won't talk.... He can't handle responsibility.'

Major John Lay, the Officer Commanding at Middle Wallop, has already pre-empted any decision about Hitch. While the course were flying to Wales, he was in a meeting with the Chief Flying Instructor. Between them, they decided he was not safe enough to be trusted on his own in the mountains. A decision about his long-term future will be made when he returns to Middle Wallop, but for the time being he mustn't be sent solo. Major Lay immediately passed this news on to Nick and now Nick is discussing it with the others.

'If you want my honest opinion,' says Sean, 'if we just come out and tell him the truth his confidence will plummet even further. We could always blame it on the weather or any other excuse.' Nick nods in agreement. But Sergeant Major Mick Pendrey disagrees: 'Whatever way you put it, he'll suss it. If he knows he's done enough to go solo and we don't send him, he'll cotton on. Maybe we should just tell him the truth, rather than trying to con the boy.' Mick's the most experienced instructor on the course and the most senior NCO. Nick and Sean may outrank him, but they respect his views and heed his advice. Nick makes a decision that they'll fly the three dual sorties with him, and if he's good enough to go solo then they'll confront him with the truth.

It's early evening by the time the instructors' conference is over, and time to check into the Ty-Mawr Hotel, just half a mile up the road from the base. This is a rare treat for them all, to be away from base on Army business and not have to stay in barracks. A holiday atmosphere pervades the group: drinks in the bar, then a shower and change into casual clothes for an evening meal of gammon or salmon. The wine flows and the conversation gets more animated. Tonight the differences in rank between instructor and trainee disappear. They're all away together and they're all looking forward to the mountains. Nick, Sean and Mick have even temporarily forgotten about the problem of Mark Hitch. Perhaps it's not surprising: this evening Mark is quieter than ever.

Tuesday, 6 December

Llanbedr, Snowdonia

This morning they discover something about the weather in Snowdonia: there's a lot of it. Sweeping clouds, showers and gusting winds drive through the valleys and up the mountains. Ten minutes later the entire scene changes and the sun appears through a break in the clouds, bathing the wintry landscape in a warm, ochre glow. It's majestic and quite breathtaking. In the middle distance sits Snowdon itself, looking dark and foreboding. Running from it are a string of valleys, with deep sharp sides, so deep that parts of the valley floor are rarely touched by sunlight.

The trainees are on their first sortie in the mountains. They're back in the right-hand seat, with the instructor on the left doing the radios and maps. This is a straightforward test of handling skills only. To begin with they're flying high, as they enter the mountain flying training area, sneaking wonderful panoramic views of the entire range. 'Fantastic', 'epic', 'amazing' – the trainees' first reactions are predictable. But they're not here to admire the scenery.

The mountain tranquillity is suddenly and brutally interrupted by the sonic boom of an RAF fast- jet scything through

The trainees have to use the wind as it swirls through the valleys; they ride the up-draughts and avoid the down-draughts. They're trying to find the path of least resistance.

the sky. It's a reminder to the humble Gazelles that they're not alone. There are all manner of military aircraft, from Tornadoes to Chinooks, practising in these mountains at the same time. And nearly all of them are bigger and more powerful than a Gazelle, so it is advisable to keep out of their way.

Descending into the valleys, the trainees get their first taste of turbulence. Nine-tenths of mountain flying is a battle with the wind: knowing where it is coming from, how it is being affected by the terrain and what is its path of least resistance. The trainees learn the set behaviour patterns of the wind as it whistles through the mountain range. On one side of a valley the wind will be heading upwards, on the other there will be a down-draught. It is a matter of using the wind rather than fighting it. They learn this by trial and error. A Gazelle may be powerful, but it's not powerful enough to rise to the top of a mountain against a howling down-draught. It's not a nice feeling to realize that you're pulling maximum power and

Take-off from the tarmac at RAE Llanbedr. It's only ten minutes' ride to the heart of the Mountain Flying Training Area.

going nowhere. Pitch settings that seemed correct back in Middle Wallop don't apply any more. Things they have taken for granted, such as hovering, assume a new complexion. 'I pulled into a hover over a pinnacle,' says an awed JP Miller, 'and it was different. You don't have any references. You're just sitting up there in the middle of nowhere with the wind swirling around you and it's very difficult to hold.'

Flying like this is exhilarating, but potentially dangerous. The trainees are taught to think over and over again about their escape procedure. They give a commentary as they fly, explaining where they're going next, how they're planning to make a manoeuvre and what they'll do in case of emergency. Bombardier Paul Stoneman is making a slow methodical approach to a ridge line. He's almost apologetic for how slow and methodical it is. 'Don't worry,' says the instructor, 'I'd rather we were slow than out of control.' After the flight Paul muses:

> Back in Middle Wallop, if the engine stops you're basically going to land on something with the surface of a bowling green. Whereas up here all you've got are these nice crunchy rocks sticking up everywhere. If you're not careful, you'll be climbing from the wreckage at the bottom of the valley.

Not all the surprises in store are unwelcome. Paul's old unit, 29 Commando, are in Snowdonia at the same time, doing their pre-Norway mountain training. He takes great delight in buzzing them while they make their way up a mountainside. 'They'll take all day to go 20 or 30 miles, whereas I cover the distance in fifteen minutes.' He laughs unsympathetically. 'They've got blisters, sore backs and piles. But there you go – you choose your job. It took me ten years to see the light!'

The first day is over. They've all flown two sorties and practised landing on pinnacles, ridges and bowls. The scale and power of the mountains has been a shock to them all. They've struggled with the wind, and learnt yet again what a difference there is between a blackboard in the classroom and the real thing. Knowing the theory of turbulence is one thing; coping with serious down-draught, forcing you 30 degrees out of kilter, is another. The two problem cases of yesterday are still not flying well. Mark and Jenny had poor

As always, a safe sortie needs meticulous planning. Mickey Rooney is attending to the details.

flights again, and both scored browns. They're now enjoying long debriefs. But they've been joined on the hit list by Corporal Nigel Harrison. He has failed today's flight and has been marked red. Mick Pendrey is furious with him and is doing his best to live up to his nickname of 'Flight Scary Monster'. He tells Nigel he obviously hasn't done his groundwork properly, his basic knowledge of wind patterns is very poor, and he's not thinking enough about escape routes. In short, Nigel Harrison gets a real dressing down. But Mick is more annoyed at Nigel's attitude than his flying ability. He thinks he's become too cocky.

From the beginning of rotary training, Nigel had a head start. He had already worked as an aircrewman, which meant he was qualified to sit alongside a pilot and at the very least be able to land the helicopter in an emergency. Furthermore, military flying is in his blood: his father is an Air Commodore, a very senior rank in the RAF, and his brothers are both jet pilots. But it has become increasingly apparent that Nigel hasn't capitalized on his initial advantage. Perhaps he was lulled into a false sense of security. He undoubtedly knew more than most at the beginning. Whatever the explanation, the others have caught up with him – slowly at first, then at a gallop – and now most of them are performing better than him. But he doesn't seem to realize it. He still acts as if he knows everything, and can cruise his way to getting his wings. Mick Pendrey's job is to disabuse him of this notion and drive home the truth: if he doesn't buck up his ideas soon, his days on the course will be numbered. Nigel takes the bollocking with his head bowed, trying to avoid direct eye contact with Mick Pendrey. It's hard to be told you're arrogant.

Dinner tonight at the Ty-Mawr is a somewhat quieter affair. There are a lot of people with things on their minds. They go to bed knowing that tomorrow, weather permitting, they may be going solo.

Wednesday, 7 December

The weather doesn't permit. There will be no solo flying today, or any flying for that matter. It's a foul day, a Snowdonia special: wind, rain, mist, hail and lightning. The trainees and instructors go through the motions of taking the helicopters out of the hangar, waiting for an up-to-date weather report, then wheeling the helicopters back again. It's only nine o'clock in the morning, but they all know, without being told, that the flying day is over.

It's time to put the bad-weather plan into action. Back to the hotel, a video for the rest of the morning, lunch and then a lecture in the afternoon. It's a big disappointment. A day in the hotel is hardly much of a substitute for another trip in the mountains. But Mickey Rooney tries to lift spirits by telling them he's also got a video of *Under Siege* for them to watch, a military fairytale of Ramboesque derring-do.

After lunch the plates are cleared and the dining room doubles as a lecture room. By now the trainees are both teachers and pupils and they're expected to give lectures to each other on various aspects of technique. Today's subject is 'the vector diagram', a key concept in aerodynamic theory. And the choice of lecturer is obvious. Nigel Harrison has boasted in the past that he knows all about vectors and aerodynamics. Now he's going to be given the chance to prove it.

'Right, first things first. I suppose everyone knows what a vector is?' Silence. The trainees are too reticent to say whether they do or not, but the instructors are less shy. 'No!' shouts Sergeant Major Pendrey, enjoying his role as puzzled student. 'Oh well, I suppose I was asking for that.' Nigel resigns himself to starting at square one, and he draws a lateral and vertical axis on the white board. He has a feeling it's going to be a long lecture.

An hour later, Nigel Harrison goes back to his seat. He's given a passable explanation of the vector diagram, and fielded all the questions posed by the instructors. Those he couldn't answer he skilfully deflected to others in the room. Nick Wharmby congratulates him on a lecture well delivered. It certainly went better than yesterday's flights.

For Nick Wharmby, the rest day also provides an opportunity to call Major Lay, the OC, with reports on the first sorties. The phone conversation is remarkably relaxed and informal. He starts with a cheery 'Hi boss...', tells him about the weather and then goes through the state of play with each trainee. Mickey Rooney and JP Miller are 'coming along nicely'. Jenny needs to be more assertive, and 'sort out the captaincy side'.

Nigel Harrison has had a good 'kick up the arse and hopefully he'll pick up from here'. And everyone else is 'doing just fine'. Well, everyone except Corporal Hitch. He then passes the phone on to Sean Dufosee, who fills in the latest on Hitch.

'He's not a happy teddy bear at the moment,' says Sean, who then goes into the grisly details. 'He said to me yesterday that he's having "the most miserable time of my life" which I find sad, given the fact that this is meant to be his career, his vocation. He's just not enjoying it.'

Sean and Nick are worried that, because of the weather, time is running out for Hitch. He'll probably manage only one more flight in the mountains before he returns to Middle Wallop to face speculation about his future on the course. If he's going to get anything out of this trip to Wales, and return in a halfway decent frame of mind, they think that it's best to talk to him now and confront him with their worries.

Major Lay agrees, adding that they should also tell him that he'll be asked to see a doctor back at Middle Wallop. Stress management,

Rain stops play. The trainees while away time in the hangar (from left to right:): Mark Hitch, Paul Stoneman, Andy James and Nigel Harrison.

on a professional level, is best left to the experts. Sean sounds relieved: 'Exactly.... There's only so far *we* can go with him'. Seeing a medic will be for his own good and will hopefully sort him out before the situation gets out of hand. Sean hands the phone back to Nick who signs off and hangs up. They look at each other with some apprehension. How should they handle the meeting with Hitch? Neither of them have been down this path before. They've encountered trainee stress before, but not to the point where they have to make psychological assessments on the mental stability of their charges. As Sean says, 'We're in the realm of Dr Freud here.'

Mark is called in for a 'friendly chat' with Nick and Sean. He fears the worst. 'Chats' in the Army have a way of being anything but friendly. An unscheduled meeting with his instructor and flight commander can only mean trouble. He enters the room hesitantly, fear on his face. Nick and Sean try hard to be friendly and dispel the tension. It's not easy. Mark is so wound up that at first he even refuses to sit down. Nick has to order him to sit down.

Mark has known for the last few weeks that the system is worried about him, and he has been mulling over his options. As he sees it, he has three choices. First, he finishes the course, qualifies as a pilot and gets to that point of blessed relief when there won't be an instructor dissecting his every move. Second, he could leave of his own volition, and return to his job on the ground. Third and last, he is tempted to follow in Jim LeCornu's footsteps and leave the course to train as an aircrewman, where the pressure is much less intense and captaincy skills are not relevant. But the problem with the latter two options is that they will both affect the one thing he is desperate for – promotion to the rank of sergeant. Now, sitting opposite Sean and Nick, it looks as if a decision has been made for him. He believes he's about to be chopped.

For the next hour Mark, Sean and Nick sit behind closed doors in deep discussion. Once Mark realizes that this isn't a firing squad, he is intensely relieved and opens up with an outpouring of emotion. He's been bottling everything up for so long. Stress is a horrible burden to bear alone and, now that the issue is out in the open, he feels that the burden has been lifted. Sean and Nick emphasize that they like him, they rate his abilities as a pilot and they're keen to see him pass the course, but the push must now come from him. Only he can sort out his career.

Mark tells them of his three choices, and Nick is sympathetic. Rather than ruling out the aircrewman option, he thinks it's a good idea. In his opinion Mark came on the course too early in terms of his emotional maturity. Two years in the less pressurized atmosphere of aircrewman training would benefit him, and then he'd still be young enough to re-apply for the pilot's course if he chose. Mark likes what he hears, but he knows that Nick can only recommend the transfer to crewman. That decision will have to be made back at Middle Wallop, by senior figures who may be less understanding.

It's not surprising that Mark spends the rest of the day in morose silence. Used to his taciturn moods, his fellow trainees don't suspect that anything is amiss. They have been kept in the dark about his problems and he certainly hasn't been keen to enlighten them. The only two people he might have told are Marcus and Jim, but neither of them are here any more.

Thursday, 8 December

The weather improves – marginally – for their last morning in the mountains. The air is wet, the cloud is low, and the visibility is poor. But it is just about flyable and everyone gets in one more flight. The officers fly first because they're in a rush to get back to Middle Wallop on urgent business – they're wanted for decoration duty at the officers' mess Christmas Ball. They all fly good last sorties, especially Jenny, who has managed to improve her approach work and is being more assertive in the air. Simon Thorn is still worried about her safety awareness, but he recognizes that she has learnt a lot in Wales and, if nothing else, she should leave here better prepared to face the challenges that lie ahead on the final phase of the training.

The NCOs also make their last flights. For Mark Hitch it is a carbon copy of the others. He is flying with his old instructor, Staff Sergeant Tony Dean, because Sean has had to return with the Christmas Ball delegation. But if the idea was to get him to open up more, then it has failed.

Mark Hitch is on his last flight in Wales. His instructor is trying to relax him, but it's not working.

He is as closed as ever. At one stage Tony compliments him on a good approach, treating him with kid gloves:

'See Mark, that wasn't too hard.... Easy-peasy-japanesy, eh?... Ma-aark?'

'Yes, Sir.... Heading 220 degrees.'

There isn't a flicker of a smile on Mark's face. There's no space left in his brain to take on board the possibility that his instructor might be cracking a joke in mid-flight.

In an effort to relax him, Tony tries to talk to Mark about his home in the Lake District, extolling the virtues of hill walking and country living. Mark nods his head in agreement, but it's only when pushed that he confirms the beauty of the area. Even then he brings the subject on to the way drugs and IRA gun-running are polluting life in Cumbria. In Mark's mind, the whole world is going wrong. Whether it's Middle Wallop or the Lake District, all that was once safe and secure is now falling apart.

By early afternoon, Course 354 have packed up their Gazelles and left Llanbedr. For Mark, Nigel and, to a lesser extent, Jenny, it's been a difficult time. For the other four it's been an exciting break from the routine. They've learnt a lot about wind and terrain, and they can safely say that they can land anywhere now. Once you've put your helicopter skids down on a snow-capped Welsh pinnacle, nothing else holds much fear. It's all a far cry from the days, a few months back, when they struggled to land in a field the size of a football pitch. They're quite sad to be going back to flat old Hampshire.

Friday, 9 December

Middle Wallop, Hampshire

Nick Wharmby is concerned. It's rare for this calm, capable young man to get ruffled, but the Mark Hitch affair is beginning to get to him. Things have escalated beyond his control.

This morning Mark had his consultation with Dr Andy Manton, the Middle Wallop Medical Officer. The conversation was, of course, confidential, but the outcome was not. The young Army doctor has recommended that Mark be grounded for the time being, to give him a chance to overcome his stress. Nick is told that Mark is unsafe to fly and suffering from severe anxiety. He interprets this as meaning that he will not be continuing on Course 354 any more. The consensus is that Hitch will now be suspended from flying training, and may try to get a place as an aircrewman or, failing that, he'll return to his previous job on the groundcrew.

But the Commandant, Colonel Mike Wawn, reads the news in an entirely different way. Corporal Hitch, he insists, has only been grounded temporarily. He will be able to resume flying some time next week. As long as he wants to carry on, there will be a place for him. As far as the Commandant is concerned, Hitch's training has already cost the Air Corps nearly quarter of a million pounds and he's reluctant to write off that money just because a man won't talk in cockpit and has a tendency toward melancholia. If he can fly, then its the instructors' job to try and ensure he passes the course. He also makes it clear that Hitch's aircrewman option is a non-starter. Corporal LeCornu had specific handling problems that they felt could be resolved by a second crack at the course after a two-year apprenticeship as a crewman. The same does not apply to Hitch. The problem is in the head, and as such it would just repeat itself if he went away and came back. The Commandant is presenting Hitch with a simple choice: stay on the course or return to the ground.

When Nick finds out what the Commandant has decided, he is understandably surprised. It's rather awkward for him, having believed that Hitch was being removed from the course, to realize that he has been given every opportunity to continue. To a certain extent, he feels that his recommendations have fallen on deaf ears. It's a reminder that, while managing the nitty gritty of the course he may be in charge, but once things get beyond a certain level there are very real limits on his power. Maybe it's a salutary lesson for a twenty-five-year-old to learn. He wanders off in search of Mark Hitch to tell him the news. He's quietly fuming.

After two hours his mood has changed completely. He has done an abrupt *volte face* just in time for the Christmas Ball. While this evening's entertainment is not as grand as the Summer Ball, it's still a fine occasion, and so it should be after all the work Sean and the other officers have put in. The mess is festooned with decorations, and there's a Christmas tree in the corner. There's a snow camouflage net suspended from the ceiling, providing the appropriate seasonal touch. And the wind section of the Corps band are playing carols. At the moment they're playing 'Silent Night'.

Again the corporals are left out in the cold. The sergeants' mess are holding their own party next week, but the four corporals in Hotspur House have nothing organized to celebrate Christmas. While the officers don black tie and tuck into turkey, they go into Andover for a take-away kebab. It's the Army way.

At the ball, the rowdiness has increased in direct proportion to the volume of noise. Most of the food has been eaten or thrown across the room. Some of the officers have emptied the helium from the balloons into their mouths and are singing carols in high-pitched voices. Others are running amok with water pistols, and in one case a water machine gun. Meanwhile Nick has slipped out and returned to his room to make another transformation, this time into Father Christmas. He and his room-mate, Charlie Pickup, will be doling out the presents that the guests have brought along. Nick stuffs a large Union Jack pillow under his costume, dons the beard and adds some dark wayfarer shades. He and Charlie look more like the Blues Brothers than Father Christmas.

With a fanfare from the trumpet and a lot of synchronized yo-ho-ho-ing, the two Santas enter the dining room. They create enough of a distraction to cause a ceasefire in the food wars. They go round the room, handing out presents to all the 'good boys and girls of Middle Wallop'. Nick makes his way over to Andy James, sits him on his knee, and asks him what he'd like for Christmas. 'A set of wings?' Andy suggests hopefully. 'No way,' chuckles Santa, as he hands him a box gift-wrapped in gold paper. Andy gives Santa a big kiss under his beard, and goes to open his present. He's not disappointed. It may not be a pair of wings, but it is a helicopter – at least a toy helicopter.

Like any child with a new toy, Andy wants to play with his helicopter straight away. He assembles the parts: pink rotor blades on to a purple fuselage, on to a turquoise handle. With a flourish he pulls the cord and hopes the helicopter will take off. But it just falls rather limply to the floor. He tries again, but when he still can't make it fly he throws it away. If only everything in life was a reliable as a Gazelle.

It would be easy to dismiss the evening as just a rollicking good time. It is certainly that. But looking at the three officers from Course 354 letting off steam after all they've been through recently, it is clear that such parties provide an important release valve. The Army Air Corps says it looks for 'stable extroverts' when selecting pilots – people who are responsible and safe, but also outgoing and forceful. And this party is what you get when you put a roomful of stable extroverts together, give them a lot to drink and take away all need for responsibility. If only Mark Hitch had a similar release valve.

Monday, 12 December

The officers have had two days to recover from their hangovers, the corporals have digested their kebabs, and Mark Hitch has made his decision. He's going to stay. He's also beginning to deny that there was ever anything wrong. He will only grudgingly admit to being 'down' – but 'definitely not miserable'. Another way of looking at it is that he may have been down but he's not out.

It's not clear whether this is evidence of a new enthusiasm for the course or a decision motivated by fear, the fear of losing his promotion if he returns to the ground. Either way he's still very much part of Course 354. Nick Wharmby greets the news with a nod and a wry smile. None of the other trainees are aware that it *is* news: the entire Hitch affair has been kept from them. They have been told that Mark is ill, but that he'll be rejoining them in a couple of days.

Mark's feelings are mixed. He knows he's now committed himself to the final phase of the training which is all about captaincy. He knows it will expose his weaknesses even further. But, against that, he's glad that at least a decision has been made and the system has supported him through this rough patch. He's in a phlegmatic mood: 'Yeah, I've had my doubts. Who hasn't? Like they keep bleating on, it's a bloody hard course. But no, I'll just keep going. I've had my fair share of ups and downs.' What is he on now, an up or a down? 'Level,' he says, deadpan, then with a smile he adds, 'flatlining!'

Monday, 19 December

It's the last day of Phase Two of Advanced Rotary. Tomorrow Course 354 break up for their Christmas holidays. There is an end-of-term mood about the crewroom. Mickey Rooney and JP are chatting about their last flights, a low-level map-reading sortie. But the mood is suddenly shattered by the latest piece of news.

'Until you've actually experienced it, you don't realize quite how quickly things can change.' Nigel Harrison was referring to the weather in Wales when he made that statement . Now, back in Middle Wallop, he appreciates how prophetic it was. Things really *have* changed: he's just been told he's been back-coursed. He'll be leaving 354 today and starting in the New Year on 355, the course seven weeks behind. He'll repeat the last seven weeks of the syllabus exercises with them and then carry on through the rest of the exercises, hopefully graduating with Course 355 seven weeks after 354.

The decision is a shock to him. 'I feel like I've been kicked in the crotch with the proverbial size nines.' Nigel is in the crew-room drinking tea and looking dazed. Mickey tries to cheer him up by telling him to look on the bright side. 'Now we'll be able to tell you the answers for all the tests coming up'. Nigel manages a weak smile. 'It's going to be hard leaving the guys on 354. We've been together for ten months and we've got quite a rapport. And it'll be strange watching them go on and collect their wings and not being there with them.' Nigel now has to go back home and tell his wife Sharon that they'll be unexpectedly extending their stay in Middle Wallop. He knows she won't be happy. She doesn't like living in the married quarters and she's been looking forward to leaving at the earliest opportunity. As Nigel says, 'It's not much of a Christmas present.'

Corporal Harrison is being back-coursed for the same reason he was criticized in Wales: his attitude. Nick Wharmby had hoped that the ticking off there would have produced a change, but Harrison has returned to Middle Wallop and the sloppiness in his flying has reappeared. Looking back over the whole course, Nick charts a consistent decline: 'He went through steady progress, to slow progress, to zero progress. And now he's having to have a whole bunch of things retaught to him, which we don't have time to do at this stage of the game.' They're using the back-coursing option as the most dramatic way of letting Harrison know that he needs to change his ways. If he's to kickstart himself on the learning curve again, then seven extra weeks of consolidation should do the trick.

At face value, the problems of Harrison and Hitch are poles apart. One is over-confident and too flip, the other is under-confident and too intense. But they are both showing symptoms of stress, the wild card in the pack of pressures the trainees face. Both have handled it badly and both have gone into a downward spiral as a result. As Nick explains:

> They're under the same pressure – in fact everyone's under the same pressure. But these two have just handled it differently. One shuts down and withdraws into himself; the other over-compensates and takes it on aggressively. He refuses to recognize there is a problem, and doesn't put in the work in the evenings. What we have to do is pull people away from the extremes on the psychological spectrum.

After ten months on the course, three trainees have been chopped, one has been back-coursed and another has had to seek medical advice. For five people out of ten to run into such serious trouble may not seem unusual on such an intensive course – until you realize they're all NCOs. All three officers are still on track. Only Andy James went on review, but he hasn't slipped up since. So, is the course biased in favour of the officers?

The unanimous answer is no. Corporals, officers and instructors alike put these statistics down to chance. 'A pilot,' says Nick Wharmby, 'is a pilot. If he's got a set of wings on his chest it doesn't matter whether he's an air trooper or a general.' An admirable sentiment. Even so, it must be more than chance or coincidence that the failure rate is so much lower for officers than NCOs. But nobody has an explanation. 'It's got nothing to do with the fact that they're NCOs,' says Andy James. 'Anyone can get chopped at any time.' Lieutenant JP Miller agrees. 'It's one of the only courses in the Army – possibly one of the only courses in the forces – that actually levels all the ranks down.' Tantalizingly, he adds that 'there are little points which we officers are expected to deal with in certain... you know, in certain ways.' But he won't be drawn on the nature of those ways. The NCOs themselves are no more forthcoming. Paul Stoneman's response is typical: 'There's no favouritism, not at all. It's purely that the ratio of NCOs to officers is higher. Everybody's proved that they've got the capability to complete the course.'

The truth of the matter is complicated. All the pleadings about equality on the course are misleading. It is true that the trainees are all taught the same way. But, away from the course, their different lives have an influence on the way they cope with the pressure. The officers' mess is a very supportive place, where the officer-trainees can share stories and problems with members of their own course and all the other courses currently going through Middle Wallop. They also mix on an informal basis with senior officers who have seen and done it all. This gives them an unquantifiable extra confidence about their prospects on the course. From day one they feel they are part of a flying community. By contrast, the corporals out in Hotspur House feel isolated. They spend their time with each other trying to sort out their flying problems, but they don't have the same sense of community, the same expectations of success.

Furthermore, since starting on Advanced Rotary and with the shift of emphasis towards captaincy skills, the officers have an inbuilt advantage: they are used to making decisions and using their initiative. The corporals suffer because they're more inclined to follow than lead, happier to take orders than to give them. Rank may be irrelevant when it comes to moving cyclic, collective and pedals, but it's not so easy for the NCOs to master all the skills that make up an aircraft commander.

It's been an interesting first three months on Advanced Rotary, but now Course 354 are parting company with Nick Wharmby. In the New Year they'll have a new flight commander for the final phase, and Nick will start with a new course back at the beginning of Advanced Rotary. The pilot factory keeps rolling on. His last task on Course 354 is to say goodbye.

He's in the briefing room with the six remaining trainees for the last time. He's upbeat and in good humour, but he also has some cautionary words for them about the final phase. 'Don't get bamboozled when they start throwing new things at you,' he urges. 'Remember the basics.' Then he proceeds to address each individual briefly, reminding them of their strengths and weaknesses. He tells Jenny to build on her assertion in the air: 'Don't let them push you over up there.' Jenny nods, rather glumly. He gives much the same advice to Paul Stoneman. He suggests that JP should guard against his natural enthusiasm: 'Try and be less gung ho.' But Andy should do the opposite: 'Be less deliberate, shave a corner or two.' For Mickey Rooney, he has nothing but praise: 'Just keep it up.' The only person he doesn't talk about is Mark Hitch. They've already had a detailed conversation beforehand. Despite last week's decision, Nick still isn't 100 per cent sure that Mark will come back in the New Year. He still finds his lack of motivation a complete mystery. Nick clearly enjoys all the paraphernalia of flying so much, he can't really understand how anyone can be so indifferent to it.

'Right, before you go, any comments?' Nick wants some feedback from the trainees.

'Yeah' says Andy James with a smile, 'you're the best flight commander we've ever had.'

Quick as a flash, Nick replies that Andy is the best pupil he's ever had. 'Apart from,' he adds, 'Corporal Rooney, Lieutenant Miller, Bombardier Stoneman... 'On the fingers of one hand, Nick ticks off every other member of the course. Everyone laughs. Then Nick looks up at Mark Hitch, sitting at the back of the classroom. 'So, how does it feel to have six weeks to go? What do you reckon, Corporal Hitch?'

Mark Hitch smiles. It's a smile that lends his eyes an air of devilment. 'I reckon we should ban all leave, Sir. Stay behind and do more flying. It's too easy, Sir.' No one's quite sure whether he is joking or not.

Chapter Six

War

Tuesday, 31 January

Fremington, Devon

'Jenny, gentlemen... we're at war!' With these words the new flight commander, Major Bruce Stewart, sends the six remaining trainees from Course 354 off to Devon. Britain has been invaded and they are going to defend the realm. Their target is the village of Fremington, near Barnstaple. This is the epicentre of the invasion.

At first glance, Fremington doesn't look like a village in the thick of things. Some lads got drunk at the local pub last night and had to be ejected by the barman. This morning the newspaper boy was later than usual delivering the papers. There was also an abnormally large traffic jam caused by faulty lights on the road to Bideford. But, other than these apparently unconnected events, all is quiet in Fremington. No one seems to know anything about an invasion.

The scene is very different at the Army camp tucked behind the parish church. Here there are maps everywhere, people are running up and down corridors carrying the latest intelligence reports, and the helicopters are ready for the off. This is Exercise Woodlark: the last set-piece exercise for Course 354 and the closest they will get to a real-life war scenario prior to winning their Wings. They arrived yesterday and took their initial recces of the area. Today they're right in the thick of it, ready to do battle with the enemy.

The enemy are the Ormidians, and they come from Ormidia, a collection of islands near the Scillies. They landed at the weekend in the picturesque fishing village of Padstow in Cornwall and now occupy the whole of the county. For years the Ormidians have been stirring up resentment among the Cornish people, playing on their Celtic roots, so the Cornish welcomed them in. They are now heading for Devon and the magnetite mines near Exmoor. Magnetite is a rare and extremely valuable mineral, which is the mainstay of the Ormidian economy. Or at least it was, until over-production in other countries, particularly Britain, forced world prices down and the Ormidians towards bankruptcy. But the Ormidians are resourceful people. They have hit upon the idea of flooding the British magnetite mines, thus pushing up prices again, and restoring their economy. In this way, they'll be teaching Britain – their historic enemy – a lesson it won't forget.

For most small islands, this plan would be a trifle ambitious. But Ormidia has help. It's a socialist republic which, since the 1970s, has aligned itself politically with the Soviet Union. It has also benefited from Soviet military equipment and technical expertise. It's a sort of Cuba in a cold climate. Glasnost or not, Ormidia is still gripped by the ideology of Marxist-Leninism.

Major Mike Scott-Hopkins, the senior tactics officer on Exercise Woodlark, is an authority on Ormidia. He's a large, enthusiastic man who has spent the last couple of years polishing and refining his knowledge of the place and its people to such an extent that he sometimes forgets that Ormidia doesn't really exist. There are no islands, no magnetite and no invasion. It's all pretend. But the challenge of Exercise Woodlark is to suspend disbelief for four days and pretend the country is at war. The trainees who can make this leap of the imagination will be the ones who come away from here with the best results.

It is unlikely, but certainly not impossible, that any of the six remaining members of Course 354 will be chopped at this late stage. What's more at issue is their potential to become aircraft commanders when they leave Middle Wallop and join operational squadrons. The ones who shine on Woodlark will be pushed on to the fast track in their new squadrons; the others will find progress after the course much slower. So a lot is riding on this one exercise, and for a month – since the Christmas holidays – they have been at Middle Wallop preparing for it. They have been working with new instructors – specialists in tactical flying – who are trying to develop their captaincy skills. They are now flying almost exclusively in the left-hand seat, concentrating on reconnaissance and observation, learning how to read a battlefield from the air, and thinking of themselves as flying tacticians. By now they know what's required of them. It's just a matter of putting it all into practice in a new and unfamiliar setting, under the simulated pressure of war.

This is the stage of the training that Jenny Firth has been most anxious about. Her previous experience had given her an advantage on the flying side, but a definite disadvantage in tactical terms. Some of her colleagues have been doing Army war game exercises for years. By contrast, her career has been spent behind a desk, with very limited battlefield practice: 'Put me in the field and ask me for a tactical situation and I have to work very hard to come up with anything sensible at all. I'm a real tactical duffer.'

Now Jenny's inexperience is catching up with her. She's been having problems with her map-reading and captaincy already, and knows that Exercise Woodlark is all about map-reading and captaincy. She is clearly worried. She has become more withdrawn and snappy, and she's forever biting her nails.

For the time being, Jenny can rest easy. There's been a hitch in the war plans, due to the Devon weather. It's so foul that the Ormidians won't come out to fight. The task of defending the realm will have to wait until the rain stops and the visibility improves. At the moment Jenny and the others are in their makeshift planning room, doing nothing much but watching the weather.

The calm is suddenly interrupted when Major Scott-Hopkins bursts into the room with his portable telephone to his ear. 'Quick, take notes.' Jenny grabs a pad. 'I'm getting reports of casualties at the following grid references...' He outlines details of a location somewhere on the A39, details that are being reported to him by his number two, Captain Rupert Hibbert, from another phone at the other end of the building. 'Right, we've been asked to get two helicopters to pick up fresh casualties and evacuate them to a field hospital.' None of the trainees is quite sure how to react: they know there aren't really any casualties, and they know they're not allowed to fly in these conditions, so what's the point of the exercise? Maybe it's a wind-up. Major Mike leaves them in no doubt – he's deadly serious. 'Come on, get going. People are dying out there!'

They go into action. Mickey Rooney and JP Miller will be the pilots and they set about planning their routes to the pick-up location. The others brave the rain and start dismantling the two Gazelles. They remove the left-hand doors, the seat, the cyclic, collective, and pedals. And in five minutes they turn the helicopters into emergency air-ambulances ready to carry a stretcher where the left-hand seat would normally be. For the weak of heart, it's a bit frightening to see how quickly a Gazelle can be dismantled. They may cost a million pounds to buy and maintain, but they can be pulled apart and put back together as easily as any Meccano toy.

When the Gazelles are ready, Mickey and JP step in and prepare to take off. Mark Hitch, as the ex-crewman, assumes the ground duties, doing the pre-flight checks for them. It is hard to say whether Mark is any more cheerful since the incident with the doctor. It is hard to say because he's hardly talking to anyone. Whatever his current state of mind, he can't really be in the best condition to tackle the demands of Woodlark. The instructors will be looking for crisp, clear instructions delivered with crisp, clear authority. It seems a lot to expect from someone suffering such inner turmoil. But, if nothing else, Mark demonstrated in Wales – and since then – a strength of will bordering on bloodymindedness. Having made the decision to stay on the course, when it would have been just as easy to leave, he is now inclined to finish it, just to prove all the doubters wrong. By a quirk of fate, he has been teamed up for the pairs sorties with Jenny. It's an odd combination. Neither are great communicators and communication is going to be of the essence. It promises to be a case of the quiet leading the taciturn.

Just before the two air-ambulances take off, Major Mike calls a halt to the proceedings. He informs them all of the new instructions he's just received. 'Casualties picked up by another patrol.... We can stand down our mission.' The trainees are not altogether surprised. They knew he'd stop them at some point in the exercise – it was just a matter of when. They cheerfully reassemble the Gazelles and return to their planning room, wondering what the next task might be.

Major Mike is not happy. He gives the trainees a good telling off for treating the exercise like holidaymakers rather than soldiers. But on this rainy afternoon, with all prospect of flying now abandoned to the weather, Course 354 can't quite share Major Mike's enthusiasm for the pretend war. It's unfortunate that Fremington has the feel of a 1950s holiday camp. When the Army Air Corps aren't here, it's used as an outdoor activity training centre. Among its nissen huts and neat lawns, there is an assault course, a pile of canoes and even a net for soldiers to practise their golf swings. It seems a long way from the frontline.

Major Mike gives up on any more fake emergencies and puts in train the alternative wet weather programme, an afternoon of lectures on related military tactics. It's disappointing to have lost a day out of the flying schedule but he's not too worried at the moment; with a long day tomorrow, they should be able to catch up. He's more concerned about the attitude of the course at the moment. They're going to have to start taking this war exercise a lot more seriously if they want to survive the dual patrols tomorrow.

Wednesday, 1 February

It's 6 a.m. and Mickey Rooney and Andy James are still in bed. They're in a three-man room in the barracks accommodation and they're showing absolutely no signs of life. The occupant of the third bed, on the other hand, is raring to go. JP Miller is already up and about, displaying his well-toned athlete's body as he washes at the basin in the corner of the room. It's unusual for two officers to share a room with an NCO, although by now Course 354 are used to the unusual. But they're not used to getting up this early. Being at war has definite disadvantages.

Mickey looks over to JP and asks enviously how he could possibly look 'like that' first thing in the morning. Andy peers at his watch and groans. 'This early malarkey,' he says, with a sigh, 'just isn't for me'. To prove the point, he disappears back under the covers. Perhaps he's hoping that the weather will interfere again and the Ormidians, being fair-weather fighters, will extend the ceasefire. But no, the forecast for today is good: lighter winds and no rain.

Their casual air hides the tension they're all feeling. They're acutely aware that in sixteen days' time there is a Wings Parade booked and they're all – 'touch wood... touch wood' – expected to be there. But it's considered bad luck to talk about it or even mention the *Macbeth* word – 'wings.' Certainly not until the small matter of Exercise Woodlark is behind them.

JP has finished dressing, made his bed and polished his boots. He leaves the room to Andy, clad in pink elephant boxer shorts and staring bleary-eyed into the shaving mirror, and Mickey who's still comatose. The two of them have become quite good friends over the last few weeks, despite the difference in rank. They were both personally taught by Nick Wharmby and they work well together. They know they'll be matched up in the pairs sorties today.

Mickey has little to fear from Woodlark. He's been flying well all the way through Advanced Rotary, and he's steered clearer of trouble than anyone on the course. If he was willing to raise the unraisable subject of wings, he'd have to admit that not only will he make it to the end, he may well make it as 'best overall student' (the top prize on the course). His only serious competition seems to be from JP. But, for the time being, he refuses to be drawn on the subject. In fact he refuses to be drawn on any subject, as he tries to snatch another ten minutes shut-eye.

Andy stands no chance of being 'best student'; at this stage he'll be grateful just to pass. But if there was a prize for 'most changed student' he would walk it. Much of his boyish naiveté at the beginning of the course has disappeared, along with his quiff. He now tries to present himself as a hard-working, serious young man responsible enough to command a patrol. In short, he's grown up over the year. But he knows there's a lot of hard work to be done before he can think about getting his wings. He still has a tendency to lose concentration at critical moments, particularly when things are new and unfa-miliar; and everything they do today will be new and unfamiliar. He's worried about how little time he'll get to prepare the flights. 'It'll mean,' he says eloquently, 'quite a lot of flapping.'

6.30 a.m. and breakfast. They're all here: the thought of eggs and bacon has lured them from their slumbers. The food is good and the helpings are generous, but the ambience leaves something to be desired. They're in a miserable catering hut on the edge of the camp, and it's still dark and cold outside. The conversation is desultory and peppered with unintelligible military-speak. In civilian life they would probably have run out of things to say to each other, but not here. Every day brings more tactical jargon to discuss.

At the same time, a convoy of vehicles is leaving the camp through the main gate. They may look like a couple of four-tonne trucks and a handful of Land-Rovers, but they are in fact the Ormidian forces. Or, rather, they are pretending to be the Ormidian forces, and they're heading off to pre-planned locations assigned by Major Mike. In the interests of greater authenticity, Captain Hibbert recently constructed a dummy tank turret and attached it to one of the vehicles to make it look more hostile when viewed through a GOA. Sadly, it blew off yesterday in the wind and was accidentally run over by one of the trucks. So today they go into the Devon countryside without any props to aid authenticity.

7 a.m. and the first pair – Jenny and Mark – are receiving their orders from Captain Hibbert at the 'command post', a bare beige office with a big map at its head. He informs them of the latest intelligence on the Ormidian advance – intelligence which has come straight from the fertile imagination of Major Mike. 'Following a series of battles during the night,' he begins, 'the enemy has failed to make further progress.... It's been reported that the enemy no longer favours the eastern axis and the all-target axis has therefore been reassessed as being Launceston to Holdsworthy.' Jenny and Mark scribble frantically in their notebooks. Pretend enemy or not, the whole thing has suddenly become horribly real.

Rupert Hibbert clears his throat as he comes to the crux of the matter. 'Mission: to report enemy in the forward battle group areas in order to assist in building an intelligence picture.' Giving the words an extra resonance, he raises his voice and repeats the mission statement. He then carries on in stentorian tones, detailing times, grid references and frequencies. Nearly all of it would mean nothing to the layperson, but Jenny and Mark seem to understand. Certainly when he asks them if they have

Jenny Firth has two weaknesses as a pilot, her map-reading and captaincy. Unfortunately, Exercise Woodlark is all about map-reading and captaincy.

any questions, they stay quiet. They're too busy scribbling. A minute later, having synchronized their watches, they go off to plan the sortie.

Jenny and Mark return to the planning room and lay out their maps on the table. It's been decided that for the purposes of this flight, Mark will be the patrol commander and Jenny his number two. On the next sortie the roles will be reversed, but for now Mark is in charge of everything that happens on the flight. He's leaning over his map trying to decipher its secrets and work out the best possible route they can take to observe the enemy without the enemy observing them. Experienced pilots can look at a map, form an instant mental picture of the topography, and identify good vantage points. But for the trainees it's a slow methodical process. There are so many things to consider: the lie of the land, the cover provided by foliage, the relative position of the sun.

They also have to bear in mind all the limitations of working on a battlefield. Until they get right up close to the enemy, they'll have to fly in areas sanctioned as safe and in friendly hands. They know that if they try and fly out of those areas they're likely to get shot down – that is, their instructors will play dead and abort the flight. Then they have to worry about their own side. They should remember that they're part of a bigger force trying to repel the Ormidians. There are supposedly units from the Royal Greenjackets, the Welsh Fusiliers and the Prince of Wales's Own Regiment providing the troops on the ground. Each of the regiments controls a section of the battlefield and has to be informed about any aircraft movement in their area.

There is also one more consideration: they have to avoid the pink blobs marked on their maps. These are no-fly zones, not for any tactical reason, but simply because they are pieces of land owned by irate Devon farmers who have complained in the past about helicopters disturbing their livestock. Respecting these no-fly zones is a number one priority, because the success of an exercise like this depends on good relations with the local community. Everything must be fed into the plan.

While Jenny and Mark are deep in thought, Andy is in another corner of the room trying to mark up his map. He and Mickey will receive their orders after the first pair have taken off. But he already looks daunted by the task. 'It's quite confusing to work it all out,' he says wearily. And indeed it does look extremely confusing. What was once a harmless map of Devon is now bristling with thick coloured lines, marked in black and blue lines. The black lines signify the boundaries of the Temporary Minimum Risk Route (TMRR), which is the main aerial pathway cleared by friendly forces and deemed to be beyond Ormidian reach. The blue lines mark the boundaries of different brigade areas. 'Every time you cross them,' Andy explains, 'you have to call them up to tell them where you're going and what you're doing.' If, that is, you know what you're doing. It's all very well drawing lines on a map, but things look different from the air, especially when you're flying low-level at speed.

Jenny and Mark's preparations are not going well. They're getting so bogged down in the details, they can't finalize a plan. Or, rather, Mark can't. He has to make a decision, and time is running out. The new Flight Sergeant Major, Tony Vaughan, will be piloting Mark's Gazelle. He's already had a word in Mark's ear, advising him that his chosen observation post will probably be a bit exposed. But Mark is struggling to think of alternatives. Jenny doesn't exactly help; she places the onus firmly on his shoulders: 'It's up to you.' Finally Mark shrugs his shoulders and makes a very uncommander-like decision: 'Oh well,' he says, 'let's just go.'

Mark briefs the instructors and within ten minutes the two Gazelles are airborne – Mark and Tony Vaughan at the front, Jenny and her instructor, Staff Sergeant Chris Lea, behind. Flying closely and in tactical formation, they leapfrog each other as they work their way across the Devon countryside. They're heading down the TMRR in the direction of the Ormidian forces, currently thought to be near Holdsworthy. Many of the fields below are flooded; there has been an excessive amount of rainfall over the past few days. It gives the scene a more apocalyptic look.

The instructors are piloting, but the patrol commander – Mark Hitch – is calling all the shots, with Jenny as his deputy passing instructions to her pilot. They're flying 'nap-of-the-earth', hugging contours and never going above 50 feet. The biggest danger at this height is the high-voltage electricity wires, which can be very hard to spot, especially when an effort has been made to landscape the pylons into the natural environment. Part of the trainees' job therefore is to keep a good lookout; there have been too many near-accidents in the recent past for anyone to be complacent.

They arrive at the Final Rendezvous (inevitably abbreviated to the FRV). This is a pre-agreed meeting place about 5 miles back from the enemy position. The two Gazelles sit in a hover together, pointing in different directions so that they can watch each other's backs. At this stage Mark radios through to the nearest ground unit for a situation report – a 'sitrep' – the latest update on the enemy. They may find that the Ormidians have moved since they received their orders. But, in this case, the enemy are still in the same position as briefed. Mark and Jenny have the green light to move off and find them.

About 5 miles away, parked in a layby near Holdsworthy, are two of the Land-Rovers and one of the four tonners which left Fremington at breakfast time. The three soldiers have covered their windscreens with sheets of material, a rudimentary but effective precaution against reflecting the sun's rays and inadvertently giving away their position. They are now sitting in one of the Land-Rovers, chatting and reading the *Daily Mirror*. It's disappointing to find that they're not listening to patriotic Ormidian music or browsing their way thorough Marxist-Leninist handbooks. But this is a pretend war, and the make-believe stretches only so far. An extra element of unreality is that – although they are playing the enemy – they are also doubling as the radio voice of the friendly forces. The Land-Rover is a makeshift communications post and keeps in constant contact with the patrol, passing on orders and information to help them. It's enough to give these part-time Ormidians a split personality.

The patrol edges its way closer to the enemy position, trying out different observation points to see which offers the best view. All the time they should be hiding from the enemy, using the contours of the land and the treeline for cover. But Tony Vaughan is not happy. 'Don't forget to talk to me. I don't know where I'm going.'

Mark looks flustered – there's so much to do. He's radioing the command post for information; he's liaising with Jenny; and he's looking at his mission analysis card for the grid references while always keeping an eye on his map, tracking the patrol's position relative to the enemy. Now Tony's asking him to talk to him more.

He tries to oblige. 'You've got sheep at twelve o'clock – a hedge to your left. A re-entrant coming north... bridge at three o'clock.' He looks at the map to check they're in the right place. They are. 'Keep your height below 50 feet. Speed below 50 knots.' Tony does what he's told, appreciating the advice. He returns the favour by giving Mark a massive hint about what he's doing wrong: 'Broaden your mind and look around. Take in the features. Don't just look at the map, look at the wider picture.'

Mark takes a good look around him, not sure what his instructor is getting at. He can tell from Tony's voice that all is not well, but he can't really ask him to spell out the problem any more than he has. Instead Mark decides to take evasive action and move on to the next observation point. So far they've been unable to spot the enemy from here. Maybe they'll have more luck from another angle.

Jenny is at a different observation point half a mile along the ridge line, scanning the horizon with the Gazelle Observation Aid, the GOA. Using its powerful magnification, she is trying to find obvious visible features and cross-reference them with her map: a farmhouse, a barn, a crossroads. She sees a small wood and looks down at her map. 'No, that can't be the right one,' she says to herself. 'It's too thick.' She keeps scanning, until she spots a tower in the distance. 'Do you think it's a pylon or a radio mast?' she asks her instructor, forgetting that Chris doesn't have the benefit of the GOA. 'I don't know, Ma'am. You tell me.' She keeps trying. Eventually he suggests they might be better moving forward and exploiting the high ground. Jenny willingly agrees and they edge further forward.

Mark has reached his new observation point. But he has a problem – he can't observe anything. There is a large spur between him and the target. But this is the position he chose in the planning room and he's going to do his best to exploit it. He asks Tony to tuck in behind some trees to the left. Tony refuses on the grounds that he'd be wasting his time: 'Hold on. You can't see even the area you're looking for from here. For us to move to those trees is going to be absolutely no use at all, is it?'

'No, Sir.'

'So what do you think we should do?'

'Find a different position.'

'Exactly.'

Once the mission is over and the patrol has landed, Mark and Jenny go straight into a debrief with the instructors. Mark reckons they managed to get a positive sighting of the enemy before the end but it wasn't confirmed. Anyway it seems small consolation when set against the problems of the sortie. 'It was shit,' Mark admits. Tony Vaughan describes it as 'poor', and goes into detail:

> On the planning side you got it together in pictorial form, but if you'd cared to look out of the cockpit on the way down, if you'd cared to open your map a bit further, you'd have seen – particularly as far as radar horizon is concerned – we were visible most of the time...

Tony then goes on to praise them for their choice of Final Rendezvous, with the caveat that it was a shade too cautious. But then, once they got into the area of operation, all caution seemed to go out the window. 'We ended up far too close to the enemy. We were within 1500 metres and a good shot with a machine gun could probably take you out at that distance.' Tony leaves Mark in no doubt that they were in the gravest danger.

He turns his attention to Jenny: 'And you, Ma'am. That was a very gutsy idea of yours.' He's referring to Jenny's suggestion that they try and make a positive sighting of the enemy by charging up the valley at speed, get in really close and charge back up another valley. It had made sense to her in the heat of battle, but now it sounded positively reckless: 'What you've got to ask yourself is does the CO want to risk you and a million pounds worth of helicopter to get the information? You've got to know how expendable you are.' The word 'expendable' has a chilling quality and, to emphasize the point, he reminds them: 'Ultimately all soldiers are expendable on a battlefield.' The trainees have a great deal of respect for Tony. They know he speaks from experience, having fought in the Gulf War with the Allied Forces. Jenny nods her head sagely, and privately resolves to do better next time. If it's any consolation, the second pair – Andy and Mickey – are performing no better.

'What frequency should we be on now?' Mickey's in a flap. He's finding it difficult to manage the radio and map simultaneously. And, to make matters worse, low cloud has descended over the high ground. Visibility is getting worse and he's finding it hard to see much through the GOA. He knows the enemy are out there somewhere, but he's going to have to move closer. As patrol commander, he makes an executive decision to head for a different observation point. Mickey looks at the map again. 'Shit... wrong fucking way.' His instructor, Staff Sergeant Rory Burnett, looks over at him and tries to reassure him, telling him to calm down.

Meanwhile Andy, the number two, is very calm. His Gazelle is sitting pretty on the side of a valley not doing very much. Andy has had a look through the GOA and decided he can't see the enemy from where he is. He's now waiting for new orders from Mickey. He's heard nothing for some time and then he realizes why. He's on the wrong radio frequency. 'Oh shit!' Two miles away Mickey is going spare. 'I've lost him. He's blind to me.'

Eventually the two helicopters re-establish contact, but by now they're running out of time to find the enemy. Mickey gives up on Andy and moves forward of the ridge to another observation point. He looks through the GOA and thinks he's got a sighting of the target. 'I guess that means,' he says doubtfully, 'we must be somewhere near the correct area.' He radios through to ground patrol and then turns to Rory:

'That was the worst sighting report I've ever sent.'

'I can't disagree.'

Back at base, Rory picks up Mickey for letting the sortie drift out of control, and blames it on poor planning. But the thrust of his criticism is levelled at Andy: 'You could see Corporal Rooney was struggling, but you didn't help him out.... It wasn't helped by forgetting your nicknumbers.' He goes on listing Andy's faults interspersing military jargon with all too plain English. 'You're lucky. If I was your patrol commander I'd have gone fucking berserk at you.' Then, just for good measure, he returns to Mickey and asks him why he didn't go fucking berserk. 'We keep telling you, forget about rank. When you're in the air you're the commander. You tell him what to do. OK?'

Mickey drops his head and nods in recognition. It's still hard for him and the other two corporals to get used to the idea that they're able – even obliged – to tick off the officers. It seems to cut so deeply against the military grain.

In the afternoon the pairs are reversed: Jenny and Andy are patrol commanders; Mark and Mickey are their number twos. But they fare little better. They seem to have learnt the lessons of the first sorties and manage not to repeat the same mistakes. They make new ones instead.

At the end of the flying day, Bruce Stewart gathers the instructors round and asks for some feedback on each trainee. None of it is very complimentary. Rory Burnett talks about Mickey's lack of attention to detail. Tony Vaughan emphasizes Mark's continued inflexibility. And Chris Lea focuses on Jenny's poor map-reading. The best flights seem to have been flown by Bombardier Paul Stoneman – who did nothing very spectacular, but at least kept out of trouble – and JP Miller, whose captaincy was excellent and would have seen him get top marks – a blue – if he hadn't tried to overload his instructor with too much detail. On today's performance he must have got a little closer to Mickey on the 'top student' stakes.

And finally the subject comes round to Andy. Bruce himself gives feedback on his flight with him, as does the OC, Major Lay, who flew the first sortie of the day with Andy:

> He was planning on the hoof all the time so the other aircraft didn't have a clue what was going on. He was totally bogged down. Everything went out the window and we got more or less lost. Tactics were a non-event; radios were a non-event. The whole thing came to a grinding halt – so we came back.

Major Lay's implication is clear. If Andy was responsible for defending the realm, the Ormidians would have been at John O'Groats by now. Bruce Stewart concurs. He describes Andy as 'lackadaisical' and 'certainly not firing on all cylinders at the moment'.

Andy is under no illusions about the day's performance. For once he's relatively subdued. He looks defeated, and sounds worried: 'It's very hard work when you're out there and you haven't got everything sorted. It's bloody annoying...' He speaks for the whole course when he tries to explain what's been so particularly stressful about today's sorties:

> You just can't plan for everything. You get out there and find you've done too much in some areas and not enough in others. It's a question of getting the balance right and when it goes wrong you feel such a biff.

He packs up his flight bag and rams his beret on to his head. 'I'm a bit gutted. I hate having shit days.' Surely it's too late for him to cock up now? 'It's never too late to cock up.'

Suppertime, and the six trainees are in the same miserable hut where they had breakfast. They're quiet – even quieter than they were this morning – and barely going through the motions of being civil to each other. Their minds are in rewind mode, working through every detail of their flights, analysing every mistake. Tomorrow they'll have one more chance to get it right.

Andy James is not finding Woodlark easy. In the Flight Commander's opinion, 'he's certainly not firing on all cylinders at the moment'.

The eight instructors, on the other hand, are ebullient. They're in the back room of the hut, cut off from the pall of gloom surrounding the course. They've supplemented their Army regulation meal with very non-regulation wine and cheese, and they're determined to enjoy their last night in Fremington. For them Woodlark is great fun, a chance to get away from Middle Wallop every seven weeks, take on the forces of Ormidia – and win every time!

Thursday, 2 February

This is the last day of the war. The trainees have until lunchtime to wrap things up if they're to get back to Middle Wallop before dark. So it's time to start inflicting some serious damage on the Ormidians. Yesterday they were merely observing them and helping with intelligence. Today they have to destroy them.

It's make-or-break day for Andy. While he didn't fail yesterday's flights, he was graded low browns on both. To avoid leaving Fremington with a reputation as a tactical ignoramus he'll have to show some definite signs of improvement today.

And, being Andy, he does. Right from the very start of the course and the early days on Fixed Wing, through to his problems at the end of Basic Rotary, he's always known how to do enough to scrape through. He has a knack of pulling out the stops when he really has to, and often when it's least expected. His flight today wasn't wonderfully good, but it was a major advance on yesterday. Most importantly, he managed the key part of the exercise: he found a good vantage point on the enemy, who were well hidden behind the post office in the village of Clawton, and he managed to call down artillery fire on to them. No, he didn't destroy a Devon village – like everything else in this pretend war, even the shells are make-believe – but he did signal through the correct grid reference that would have scored a direct hit if there had been a real artillery battery in attendance. The procedure reminded him of the day on the range at Salisbury Plain. The skills learnt there, liaising with the gunners, were being replicated here – minus the high explosive.

After the flight Andy knows it has gone well and he looks relieved. He discusses the sortie with his partner Mickey, dwelling on the moment when they couldn't get radio contact with the command post: 'I was getting really stressed and so embarrassed, knowing they were going to think I'm such a biff.' But, biff or not, he's off the hook. Bruce Stewart debriefs him and gives him a clean bill of health. Andy may not have come out of Woodlark with a reputation as a tactical whizz kid, but he's survived.

The same can be said of Jenny, who also flew this morning as a patrol commander. After a rather limp performance yesterday, she made a conscious attempt to be more decisive, talking more with her instructor and the other Gazelle. Her observation positions were good and, like Andy, she easily managed to find the enemy and bring down fire. Her instructor looks pleased as he signs off from the target area: 'Two enemy tanks burning and retreating to the east.' But Jenny is more sceptical: 'When we get back they'll probably say I got the wrong target, and destroyed an electricity van and an Iceland lorry.' They both laugh, satisfied with a successful mission.

Back at Fremington, the other trainees are already dismantling their war HQ and loading up the Gazelles for the flight back to Middle Wallop. Major Mike gives his verdict on the exercise: 'It's been a success. The students have learned an awful lot in this testing countryside. I hope they've enjoyed it.' And the latest state of hostilities? 'I think we've won. The Ormidians have been brought to a halt, pending negotiations for their withdrawal.' He breaks into a smile, the first hint he has given that the war might be anything but deadly serious. The Ormidians can now return to their socialist hideaway in the Atlantic, ready to return in seven weeks' time

Andy prepares to return to Middle Wallop. He's not looking forward to the journey, because he's been made to fly in a chemical warfare contamination suit. Such are the hardships of war!

when the next set of trainees – Course 355 – attempt Exercise Woodlark.

Andy comes out of his final debrief and wanders back to the planning room to pack up his things. As he passes Tony Vaughan in the corridor, Tony gives him a malicious smile and tells him there's a little surprise on his desk. Andy knows enough about the ways of the military to know that 'little surprises' left on desks are not usually nice little surprises. And so it proves. Laid out by his maps is a full Nuclear Biological and Chemical contamination suit, the sort issued but not used in the Gulf War. Whether it is intended as a reward or punishment is not clear. Andy is going to have to fly back to Middle Wallop with this on for the sake of extra realism. He sighs. It's been hard enough over the last couple of days; does he really need this?

He reluctantly gets kitted up: overalls first; then smock, gloves and mask. The suit is made of a thick green fibre impregnated with granular activated carbon and is resistant to all contamination. It must be a great comfort to soldiers facing a potential chemical attack, but for this trainee pilot in the backwaters of Devon it's a major inconvenience. It's hot, heavy and very cumbersome. He waddles out to the Gazelle looking part deep-sea diver, part alien. He starts up the helicopter and takes off. 'It was a nightmare, to be honest,' Andy recalls later, 'I had the window open but it didn't make a lot of difference. And your vision is obscured by those two little glass portholes in the mask.' The awkwardness of flying for two hours in a helicopter wearing all this garb is only offset by the thought that Middle Wallop beckons. At least Woodlark is over.

Thursday, 9 February

Middle Wallop, Hampshire

It's been a strange week. No more rigid timetables, no more classes to attend. Instead the emphasis has been on revision. Each trainee has been receiving instruction tailored to their particular areas of weakness, while at the same time recapping on some general handling skills. It's been hard work, as well as rather alarming to realize how much they've both learned and forgotten.

And still no one dares talk about the Wings Parade, now only a week away. They haven't even sent out their invitations yet; they don't want to tempt fate. Everything could still go horribly wrong. They're all troubled by the story of a pilot a few courses back who got chopped a day before his Wings Parade. Whether the story is entirely true or not matters little; it has taken on apocryphal status. It's a morality tale with a simple message: 'Don't count your chickens...'

The last obstacle between the trainees and their wings is the Final Handling Test (FHT). They've already done two other FHTs – at the end of Fixed Wing and Basic Rotary – but this is the final Final Handling Test. Again, this FHT is meant to be a formality, a way for the military to put all the ticks in the right boxes and confirm that each trainee has reached the required standard. Again, the trainees find it impossible to think of it as such. Their whole careers seem to be resting on this one flight. A failure here would be terminal.

But one by one they pass. First down are Mickey and JP, the top two trainees on the course. Mickey has recovered from a rather indifferent display at Woodlark to fly a very good FHT, despite the conditions: 'That was the worst weather I've ever flown in!' JP has also cruised through the last hurdle. He can't quite believe it, but he's now a qualified Army pilot: 'One of the instructors came up to me afterwards and said "Welcome to the club" and I suddenly thought, my God you've made it – by the skin of your teeth maybe – but you've made it.' Mickey Rooney is similarly delighted: 'I'm chuffed to bits!'

Now they're waiting in the crewroom at the back of the hangar for the next of their number to complete the test. As soon as they see the expression on his face they know it's good news: Andy is hopeless at disguising his emotions. He's grinning manically and punches the air as he enters the room: 'Y-e-s!' Mickey Rooney suggests that they might be having a drink or two tonight, and Andy tends to agree: 'Just one or two...'

He tells Mickey that during the FHT he fell for 'a classic'. The instructor asked him to point out the fire warning caption on the Gazelle's instrument console. Privately he wasn't very sure but pointed confidently to the third button from the left on the top row. The examiner asked him if he was certain. He reconsidered and decided it was in the top right corner. Then the examiner quizzed him on the correct procedure when the caption came on. Again Andy wasn't sure but he gave what he reckoned was a fairly convincing answer. The examiner offered him the chance to think again, but this time Andy stood by his answer. 'That's a pity,' said the examiner, 'because there isn't a fire warning caption in the Gazelle.' Mickey listens to Andy's story but doesn't laugh at the punchline. From the expression on his face it's clear that he didn't know about the fire warning caption either. Andy disappears for a 'celebratory fag'.

Next down is Jenny. As soon as she comes out of her debrief, her instructor congratulates her. He's been pacing up and down the hangar like an expectant father, waiting nervously. When he hears the good news he is delighted and a little relieved. In fact he looks more excited than Jenny, who seems to be taking it all in her stride. Rather than hang around with the others, basking in the glory of their success, she is more concerned about going back home and feeding her new labrador puppy. She is obviously happy to have finished, but she claims she's 'just not the sort of person that's going to jump and down and start screaming about things. I've managed to do what I wanted and that's fine.'

Mark Hitch has been ill and should be sitting the test tomorrow, so there's only one more person to land today, Paul Stoneman. When he comes down and finishes his debrief he enters the crewroom, giving nothing away. So they ask him how it went. 'Oh he failed me,' replies Paul matter-of-factly. They don't believe him; they know he has the driest sense of humour on the course. They demand to know the truth, but he assures them he's failed.

When they realize he's not winding them up, they are horrified and pile on the sympathy. Jenny asks if there's anything she can do to help. Paul looks sad for a moment and says, 'Yes there is actually.' Jenny leans forward and asks what. Paul keeps a straight face and explains: 'The windows in my flat are dirty, you wouldn't like to clean them, would you?' They all laugh, impressed by how calm Paul seems to be. If he's not worried they won't worry for him. So they go off to start what Mickey promises will be a 'week of solid drinking'. Paul and Mark Hitch can catch them up when they pass tomorrow.

Friday, 10 February

Mark Hitch is feeling better this morning and is well enough to sit his FHT. Soon afterwards he feels ill again – he fails. But this setback is overshadowed by the news that Paul Stoneman has also failed, for the second time.

When word of this filters through to the crewroom, the others are shocked, but they also feel strangely vindicated. They knew it was never over 'until the fat lady sings...' and other such clichés, and now, with these two crises, they've been proved right. It really is a hard course and nothing can ever be taken for granted. So much for FHTs being a formality. Course 354 is going down to the wire.

This is new territory for the system. They're not used to seeing two people fail their FHT on the same course. With Mark the solution is clear: he'll re-sit on Monday. But with Paul they are uncertain. They've decided to let him have a second re-sit on Monday, this time flown with the Chief Flying Instructor (CFI). But, if he fails that, no one knows what they'll do. Allow him to keep re-sitting until he passes? Not a good idea, because he obviously doesn't perform well in tests. Put him on review? Possibly, but there might not be time to complete the extra hours before Wings. Back-course him like Nigel Harrison? Disruptive for the course behind. Chop him? A very drastic step, given that he's passed all the other hurdles satisfactorily. To be honest, they're just hoping he passes on Monday. Then the problem will be solved.

Paul himself has been hit by the failure. Yesterday's stoicism has given way to shock. The prospect of wiping out a whole year's work in one flight is too awful to consider, but he can't stop considering it. He goes into a meeting with Major Lay, obviously distressed with the situation. By the end of the meeting he can barely speak. Everyone else on the course is speaking in whispers.

Monday, 13 February

Paul and Mark don't elaborate much on their respective weekends. But nobody has much difficulty imagining what they've been going through.

The last days at Middle Wallop are spent in the air. The course is nearly over, but there's the small matter of the Final Handling Test to overcome.

Paul has been back in Poole with his wife Julie. At the beginning of the course they made a conscious decision to live apart during the week. She stays in their smart red-brick home with their baby daughter and he lives in Hotspur House. They thought this would be a good way of cutting out distractions and allowing him to concentrate on his flying. But this weekend she's had the job of nurturing him through this crisis and sending him back to Middle Wallop in a better state of mind. For two days, she's helped him dismiss all thoughts of 'what if...' and placed complete faith in his ability. Now Paul has to have the same faith in himself. This morning he marches determinedly out to the helicopter and prepares to take off. The CFI soon joins him.

Mark, on the other hand, has been stuck in Middle Wallop all weekend, trying to avoid the revellers. He's spent most of the time in his room, waiting for the hours to tick by. Now, as he walks out to his Gazelle, he's so preoccupied he doesn't seem to realize when one of his maps blows away from under his arm. A few paces further on, a second one blows away but he still doesn't notice. It's only when he gets into the cockpit and starts looking for them that he sees what's happened and scurries off to retrieve them. He returns to the helicopter and readies himself for his examiner, the Deputy CFI.

Different examiners, different results. An hour later the flights are over and, much to everyone's relief, the drama is over. Mark and Paul have both passed. Trainees and instructors are delighted. Paul jumps into the air with relief, dances a quick jig and smiles to himself: 'Cinders, you shall go to the ball.' He heads off to ring up his wife and tell her the news. Mark Hitch is just as happy: 'Anyone want some maps?' he asks as he breezes into the crewroom, 'because I'm not going to fucking need them ever again!' He can barely restrain himself from rushing straight out and catching up on three days missed drinking time. But he knows there's still business to attend to. He's been summoned to see Major Lay.

Mark marches in, and from the look on the OC's face he is not happy. Surely Mark isn't going to get another bollocking? Surely they can't take away his wings before he's even got them? The OC launches into a ticking-off: 'Corporal Hitch you've been giving me a lot of grief recently....' Mark looks uneasily at the Major. 'And I have some bad news for you – you're improperly dressed.' Mark stares back, uncomprehending. Then the Major smiles, picks something up from his desk and hands it to Mark. 'Here, sew these on, Sergeant Hitch. Congratulations.' Mark is stunned. He can't think of anything to say beyond 'Thank you, Sir.' Then he stares in disbelief at the sergeant's stripe in his hand, salutes and leaves the room.

It's been quite a day for Mark. He started it as a trainee corporal pilot, having to re-sit his FHT, uncertain of his future. He ends it a qualified sergeant pilot. Wings and promotion in the same day – it's a heady mixture. With the combination of a sergeant's salary, plus the qualified pilot's extra flying allowance, his pay has nearly doubled in one day. 'When you consider the problems I had during the course, it's definitely special to pass; without a shadow of a doubt.... And the extra bonus, a sergeant's stripe.' Now he really does have cause for celebration.

Wednesday, 15 February

Course 354 face their last challenge, how to leave their mark for posterity. Every course contributes something to the walls of the Advanced Rotary crewroom. There are bits of helicopters: rotor blades, skids and a fenestron. There are items of furniture, books and plaques. One of the recent courses left an oversized pair of *papier maché* breasts. But most courses leave photographs of themselves in bizarre poses. One group dressed up with condoms on their heads; another wore sanitary towels attached to their flying suits. The most outrageous were the group who posed wearing nothing but helmets and birthday suits, with their flight reference cards covering their genitalia.

The six members of 354 want something more dignified, something classier. They've opted for a group photograph with no hint of lavatorial humour. Everyone else at Middle Wallop calls them the Hollywood Course so they've decided to act the part. Against the backdrop of the Middle Wallop control tower, they're now lining up in profile for the camera. They're dressed in tuxedos and black tie, each of them holding a fake Oscar. The photographer tells them to look dreamy, and he releases the shutter. Snap. Six film stars immortalized on celluloid.

It's been a tough year for these six – and the four who haven't made it this far. The instructors regard it as a below average course: a normal failure rate might have been 20 per cent – two out of ten. To have lost four is unusual. In fact, two of the failures – Jim LeCornu and Nigel Harrison – will get another chance to complete the course at a later date, so the figures aren't as bad as they might appear. But there is still a consensus that things haven't gone well.

A variety of reasons are offered in the bars and crewrooms of Middle Wallop: there were too many training risks included in the original ten; there wasn't enough team spirit; people became too isolated and introspective; there wasn't a single strong unifying figure in the group; the senior NCO, who could have played the pivotal role, was the first to be chopped. Everyone has their own explanation, and the truth is probably an amalgam of them all. Whatever the reason, 354 will not be remembered in the annals of the Army Air Corps as one of the best courses.

However, it will be remembered: 354 is the first course to have been featured in a television series. Some have enjoyed being in the spotlight, others have shied away from it, but they've all had to make some adjustments to fit in around the demands of the filming. The pressure of being watched by instructor *and* camera must have had an effect on the course and may have contributed to their below-average performance.

But this is no time for postmortems. The six film stars clutching their Oscars to their hearts are more interested in looking forward now. From Friday they'll be leaving Middle Wallop and joining their new squadrons. Careers as Army pilots beckon, but first the small matter of a three-by-one-inch cloth badge that needs pinning to their uniforms. They've dreaded saying the word, but now it's safe. In two days' time they get their wings.

Friday, 17 February

It seemed this day would never come. Yet suddenly it's here. Polish the boots and practise the salutes – at 12.30 p.m. six new army pilots pass out. They already know they've qualified but today they make it public, in front of friends, families and instructors – everyone who has shared their highs and lows over the last twelve months. People have travelled from all over the country to be here. Mickey Rooney's family have come down from Scotland for the day, but his father has made an even longer journey. He works as an English teacher in Peru and he's flown over specially for the event.

But, rather than feeling relieved, the six members of Course 354 are nervous – perhaps as nervous as at any moment during their training. These are the normal nerves of a wings presentation, made worse because 354 have been awarded a great honour. They will be receiving their wings from General Sir Charles Guthrie, the Chief of the General Staff. He is the most senior officer in the Army and his presence at Middle Wallop is akin to a royal visit.

The parades are normally held in the hangar, but this one has been moved to grander surroundings at the Museum of Army Flying. A clearing has been made within the collection of old planes and helicopters and a stack of chairs have been imported and arranged with military precision. At the front there's a line of armchairs, commandeered from one of the crewrooms. They're not exactly smart, but they will at least make the General's wife and other dignitaries a little more comfortable.

At the moment the General hasn't yet arrived, so the trainees have a bit more time to polish their boots, brush down their service dress and practise their salutes. The fifty-strong party of family and friends are being shown a video, explaining what the course is all about. Half of them have lived and breathed helicopters for twelve months and feel they're almost qualified to fly them. Others, however, are transfixed by the scenes of flying, the discomforts of the survival training, and the sheer volume of skills and information that their loved ones have been learning.

Andy's girlfriend Vanessa definitely falls into the first category. She has become something of a feature of Middle Wallop parties over the past few months, and something of an expert on helicopters. She has a helicopter identification chart on the bathroom door of her London flat and is now a self-confessed 'helicopter bore'. Mark Hitch's fiancée Heather falls into the latter category. Living in Cumbria, she hasn't been able to visit Middle Wallop until now. All she knows about the course are the scraps that Mark has passed on during trips back home. But she's obviously learnt something over the year, because she's baked a cake for the occasion, decorated with a perfect icing likeness of a Gazelle.

By 12.30 p.m. the video is over and the guests have been ushered to their seats in the museum. The band strikes up the Army Air Corps march and Jenny leads Course 354 on to parade. They reach their positions and come to an abrupt halt, lining up in order of rank: Jenny first; then JP and Andy; followed by the newly promoted Sergeant Hitch,Paul Stoneman and finally Mickey Rooney. They are standing in front of a vast diorama depicting the Normandy D-Day landings. It's a fitting if somewhat bizarre backdrop. Once the group are static and the

Two proud Army pilots accept their awards from General Guthrie. For Jenny Firth (left) and Mark Hitch (right) it is the end of a long year.

first batch of photographs has been taken, the band stops, the guests rise to their feet, and General Guthrie makes his entrance. Looking resplendent in a khaki uniform dripping with gold braid, he takes up a position in front and to the side of the course. Jenny marches over to him, salutes and declares the group ready for the presentation. She then marches back and resumes her position in the line. The six of them look so serious and scared. This is much more frightening than taking on marauding Ormidian hordes.

Major Lay is standing behind the General and announces the first student: 'Lieutenant Jenny Firth, posted to 3 Regiment Wattisham.' Jenny steps forward and marches grimly up to the General for a second time. They swap salutes and the General offers his congratulations. His words are for her ears only; his rich, fruity voice is lowered to confiding tones. Then a soldier

approaches from the side, carrying a small tray. Sitting on the tray are six new pairs of wings. The General picks one up and places it it on Jenny's uniform over a newly sewn strip of velcro. He lets go and the wings stay there. Jenny is a pilot. They then turn to the photographer and a picture is taken for posterity. Jenny marches back to her place, relieved, proud and a little less grim.

'Lieutenant John Paul Miller posted to 4 Regiment Wattisham.' JP is so nervous that his approach to the General is more of an angry stomp than a march. His face is set in a grimace as he salutes. But the General is used to people being nervous in his presence and he doesn't bat an eyelid. He takes the second pair of wings from the tray and attaches them to JP's chest. Again a photograph is taken and JP returns to the group.

The process is repeated with the other four trainees. 'Second Lieutenant Andy James posted to 5 Regiment Northern Ireland... Sergeant Mark Hitch posted to 4 Regiment Wattisham... Bombardier Paul Stoneman posted to 4 Regiment Wattisham... Corporal David Rooney posted to 5 Regiment Northern Ireland.' They all look apprehensive: happy just to be able to march their few paces to the General, say a few words and march back without making fools of themselves. The only comic note is the reminder that Mickey isn't really a 'Mickey' at all – he's a 'David'.

The whole process has taken just five minutes from start to finish. It's probably been the longest five minutes of the year. Major Lay adds with a flourish: 'Ladies and gentlemen, Army Pilot's Course 354,' which is a cue for thunderous applause from all the guests.

The look of pride on the faces of parents, spouses and friends is obvious. They're clapping their hands as if their lives depended on it. But there is one face which stands out as pensive and not a little sad. It's the face of a man who wishes he wasn't sitting here in the sixth row of the audience, but standing up there in front of the D-Day diorama. It's the face of Corporal Marcus Lock.

Why on earth has Marcus come and put himself through the emotional pain of witnessing 'what might have been'? He shrugs and smiles wistfully: 'I just wanted to see the lads. It's a big day for them, I wanted to congratulate them. It means a lot to me.' It must mean a lot. He has come all the way from his infantry base in Germany. 'After I was chopped,' he says bitterly, 'they asked me where I wanted to go. I told them the one place I *didn't* want to go was Germany. And that's where they sent me.'

Since resuming his infantry career, Marcus finds himself lacking self-motivation. Interestingly, he has turned up today in a regular dark lounge suit, wearing nothing to give him away as a soldier. He's desperate to be posted back to England nearer his fiancée Angela, and equally desperate to find a way of returning to the Army Air Corps. He's still chasing his dream of becoming a crewman and one day getting another stab at the pilot's course. 'I love helicopters and I'd love to go back to flying. It'd be brilliant.' At the moment the Corps are holding out no hope of the transfer ever being granted.

Marcus's fate seems all the sadder when compared to that of another of today's guests, Corporal Jim LeCornu. In contrast to Marcus, he's turned up in Army Air Corps service dress, full of the joys of life. It is amazing what a few months away from the pilot's course can do. Since starting his aircrewman training, Jim is looking so much more cheerful and positive than at any point during his eight months on 354.

Corporal Nigel Harrison is also more cheerful. Things are going well for him on 355, and the shock tactic of back-coursing him seems to have worked. He is here at the ceremony today with the others from 355 on clear-up duty. In fact, strictly speaking, he should have been playing a key role in the proceedings. The tray-bearer's job is meant to go to an Army Air Corps corporal from the course below, and Nigel is the only Army Air Corps corporal in 355. But the authorities decided it was just too insensitive to ask him to carry the wings for his former colleagues. So an NCO from another regiment was chosen and Nigel was left to watch from the side. He can look forward to another Wings Parade soon – his own.

The only member of the original ten not here is Staff Sergeant Mark Finch. He is still with the Royal Signals in Northern Ireland, on exercise at the moment and therefore regretfully unable to make the trip. Mark has come to terms with the fact that he'll never fly again. And he's resumed his Signals career in good humour while he considers his long-term future. He still has his flat in Andover and, whenever he uses it at holiday times, he looks up the others on the course and catches up on Middle Wallop gossip.

The General is now handing out the prizes. Speculation about who has come out on top of the pile is about to end. First, Jenny receives an award for achieving the best examination results. Then JP is declared best student on Fixed Wing. He's smiling now and the smile broadens when he finds out that he's also best student on Basic Rotary. He's wondering – as is everyone else – if it's going to be three in a row. But no, the final award – best overall student on Course 354 – goes to Mickey Rooney. He's delighted, but, like the other award winners before him, he has to give his prize straight back. He holds the trophy in his hands for all of twenty seconds, just enough time for a quick photograph.

The clapping dies down and the audience look on expectantly as General Guthrie clears his throat and begins a speech. He starts by congratulating the trainees on passing one of the most demanding courses in the British Army: 'You have achieved a very great deal and you should be rightly proud of what you have done.' Suddenly it's beginning to sink in. They are ready to fly out tomorrow and take a helicopter into a war zone, anywhere in the world. The General goes on:

> In all the recent conflicts, the helicopter has more than proved its worth. With a new generation of even more sophisticated army helicopters only a few years away, your flying skills will become even more important to the Armed Forces. They will make significant changes to the way the army goes about its business, both on the battlefield and in support of peace. They will lead the way.

A single Gazelle is cutting a swathe through the blue skies over Middle Wallop. The business part of the day is over; now the flying display can begin. The champagne is flowing and the trainees – correction, pilots – from Course 354 are spending some time with their guests.

Mickey Rooney is with his parents. He touches his wings as if he still can't believe they're there: 'This is the culmination of everything I've wanted to do for twenty-three years. I've never wanted to be anything else bar a pilot. What else is there? It's the best job in the world!' Having been in Peru, his father hasn't

Ten soldiers started Course 354, only six of them have become pilots. Back row, from left: Bombardier Paul Stoneman, Second Lieutenant Andy James, Sergeant Mark Hitch. Front row: Lieutenant JP Miller, Corporal David Rooney, the Chief of General Staff, Lieutenant Jenny Firth, Corporal John Bedborough (from Course 353).

seen him all year. He can't believe how much the course has changed his son. 'He's so much more responsible and self-confident. He's no longer a kid.' Mickey will be staying on at Middle Wallop to do a conversion course on to the Lynx helicopter. He'll then be posted to Northern Ireland for two years. Like everyone else, he's uncertain what the role for helicopters will be, in the light of the ceasefire. 'Apparently they're still doing a lot of flying, so that's the main thing. Just because Ireland's gone quiet, it doesn't mean there won't still be plenty for us to do.'

Andy James is also heading for Northern Ireland, on a two-year Gazelle posting. He and Mickey will eventually team up together, hopefully with better results than they managed on Exercise Woodlark. At the moment Andy is leaning against the museum's prize possession – an Argentinian Huey captured during the Falklands War – telling Vanessa what it felt like to receive his wings. 'My leg was shaking uncontrollably. I mean it was the Chief of the General Staff wasn't it! It wasn't just any old general.... But it's been a great day. Something we've been waiting a year for. Oh God, we're so lucky!' Vanessa is tickled pink for him, but her smiles hide a sadness. She's upset that Andy will be away for so long. It's been hard enough conducting a relationship all this time between Middle Wallop and London. It'll be even harder with Andy in Northern Ireland for two years.

JP is smiling as he watches the display. He wants to savour his last hour at Middle Wallop. Like the others, his departure is imminent and his short-term future has been decided. 'I'm going to stay on Gazelle, and I'll probably join an anti-tank squadron as a recce pilot.' After that anything could happen. JP goes on to explain that a trainee from the course above them went into the same regiment after qualifying, and has now been sent to Bosnia. Although the role in Bosnia is obviously a peacekeeping one, JP stresses that it's a potentially dangerous environment. 'We're trained for the unexpected. We could be sent anywhere in the world to do any kind of job.' He knows that real enemies will be much harder to deal with than pretend Ormidians.

Paul is with his wife Julie, looking a lot happier than he did this time a week ago. 'I've been on some high pressure courses before and that's held me in good stead, but the last few days have been something else: a bit of a do or die situation.' Having failed two FHTs, he has been subjected to the most intense stress. He's only just recovering. But now he has qualified he can look ahead. 'I want to get on to the attack helicopter programme – that was one of my motivations for coming here in the first place. With the attack helicopter and all those missiles and sidewinders, you can really kick ass.' Paul, the commando, is the only one who positively seems to relish the thought of taking a helicopter into battle. He's found Middle Wallop and flying Gazelles a bit tame. He's used to life on the frontline.

Jenny is standing next to husband Steve. She has every right to look pleased, she's only the fourth woman ever to have passed out as an Army pilot. Yet she doesn't give the impression of someone whose greatest wish has just come true. For her it seems to be just another goal achieved, and she's not sure whether she wants to take it much further. The stress of the course, particularly over the last few months, seems to have diminished her desire to fly. She's now required to do three years with the Army Air Corps, in return for the investment they have put into her, but she has no ambitions to stay on once that time has expired. 'I'm quite satisfied,' she explains succinctly, 'that I'm able to give the Air Corps the commitment they expect. Then my time will be up and I'll be expected to leave.' Jenny started the course as one of the great dreamers, fuelled by a passion she has had from childhood. She ends it as one of the arch pragmatists.

'I hated it. I hated every bit of it.' To call Mark Hitch a pragmatist would be missing the point. His feelings can best be described as fear and loathing, and now the course is over he's prepared to admit it. He can't stand the 'Wallopisms', by which he means the constant assessment and criticism that goes on every day in the name of training. It's destroyed every last vestige of enjoyment he might have got from flying. When asked whether there was any moment on the course he enjoyed, he thinks for a moment and says, 'Survival week.' Why? 'Because it didn't involve any flying!'

And the future for Mark? After his problems on the course, he'll be sent to Wattisham in Suffolk – the same base as Jenny, his Woodlark partner. But, unlike Jenny, he won't progress on to Lynx. He'll stay on Gazelles, and keep in the slow lane. He's hoping that, without the pressure of the course, he will settle down and warm to the idea of flying as a living. 'I've earned the right to go to a unit. I'm sure I'll enjoy the job from now on because I'll be in a squadron away from Middle Wallop.' Maybe. Unfortunately for Mark the learning curve doesn't stop here. He'll carry on being assessed throughout his flying career. For Army pilots, pressure is an occupational hazard.

The six graduates of the course have had their last group photograph taken and are now standing together watching the flying display. These are their last few moments at Middle Wallop, before they part company and start their new jobs. They're not sure how to say goodbye or find the words to sum up their emotions. So they say nothing and look to the skies instead.

The Gazelle suddenly heads into a nose dive. It looks for all the world as if it's going to crash. Then it turns nimbly and begins to climb again. It soars high into the sky before it stops and pirouettes as gracefully as any ballet dancer. It's a display of breathtaking virtuosity and Mickey, Andy, JP, Jenny, Paul and Mark can only watch in awe. Eventually the silence is broken by Mickey. His voice is almost a whisper and he's addressing no one in particular. 'You can do anything with a helicopter. Absolutely anything. That's what the Army's suddenly realized, isn't it?'

Index